*Combating Ignorance and Powerlessness*

*Combating Ignorance and Powerlessness*

# Combating Ignorance and Powerlessness

**Milton Franklin: Author**
**Yolanda Franklin: Editor in Chief**
**Nigel Franklin: Editor**
**Milton Franklin Jr: Illustrator**

*Combating Ignorance and Powerlessness*

ISBN 1627190015
Combating Ignorance and Powerlessness
Milton Franklin, Author
Yolanda Franklin, Editor in Chief
Nigel Franklin, Editor
Published by the International Center for Intellectual Development
Nigel Franklin, President
Milton Franklin Jr., Art Work/Cover Design, Illustrator

# In Gratitude

Your purchase of this book constitutes a direct contribution to the Center for Intellectual Development, and the work this organization is conducting to advance the right to happiness of everyone that shares this planet, and we thank you. This fundraising effort will go on indefinitely as we attempt to improve the lives of women and children everywhere. Join us in this effort as we attempt to create a new world for all those who wish to live in peace, and to do good.

*Milton Franklin*

*Combating Ignorance and Powerlessness*

**Table of Contents**

*Combating Ignorance and Powerlessness*

# DEDICATION

This book is dedicated to the men and women of all ages who dare to think, standing up to the onslaught of intimidation perpetually unleashed by the mindless dogma driven individuals in all countries. The simple yet powerful statement being made by this writing is that the era of intimidation is over. The gathering of thinkers that this book represents, is a process that makes no apologies for the ideas it advances, and it will stop at nothing to empower those who dare to think.

Thinkers of all ages willing to practice intellectual honesty by going where their thoughts take them will find a welcoming home in our organization, The Franklin Center for Intellectual Development. It is the organized body on which we depend for carrying forth the simple idea that the loud mouths and intimidators no longer control the conversation between humans.

*Combating Ignorance and Powerlessness*

# INTRODUCTION

Over the years I've attempted to write, documenting ideas I know will be helpful in advancing the species, most particularly ideas that could advance members of the cultural, ethnic or racial group I happen to be a part of. These were rather minor personal projects, none rising to the level of published work. This particular work, and the one accompanying it specifically on the subject of addiction; are different in nature. They are the first of a series of books projected to be published, and distributed by The Franklin Publishing Company. This particular publication is the result of some extensive research in a rather intense master's program completed a few years ago. Some of the papers were written using the Chicago format, and others were completed using the California format, but the vast majority of the research writing for that psychology master's program was conducted in a format suggested by the American Psychological Association. The APA format is useful for academic work but no writer will restrict himself to the limitations of that format. The research itself was conducted over a period of three years but it was preceded by more than thirty years of organizational and intellectual activities on a range of subjects designed to alter the socioeconomic conditions of some of the most marginalized people on the planet. Powerlessness in all of its painful ramifications will be explored in detail beginning with the child and the horrifying treatment we have as a species meted out to the most vulnerable among us.

Dianne Ravitch wrote a book in which she chronicled the history of education in the United States starting with the city of New York. In it, we get a clear picture of how the city itself developed from a slum predominated area, to the metropolis it was to become a few decades later. What was most fascinating about the book however was the biographical piece in which she described her own journey towards a PhD. Ravitch (1988) gives us a compelling personal story of raising young children while pursuing her academic goals and about the illness and death of one of these. Ravitch was in the process of seeking a publisher for the book she was working on at the time while raising two young children. The book was to be called *The Great School Wars,* an account of the historical struggles within the history of the New York City public school system. Ravitch's (1988) intriguing story of how she was able to talk her way into a PhD program without having done a single credit at the master's level is inspiring. Without a master's degree, it was made clear to her that she would not be accepted into the PhD program, but she persevered, enlisting the assistance of faculty members at the University with whom she had already enjoyed a long friendship. The history department at the university turned her down flat, pointing to her  age and her gender as added reasons why she would not be accepted, in addition to that of not having a master's. The faculty member whom she had a long standing friendship with went by the name of Cremin, and he gave her some hope that she could enter the doctoral program in history at the Columbia School of Arts and Sciences and that he would make sure most of her courses were with him. Also to her good fortune, her friend Cremin ran the dissertation seminar, and he made it clear to her that she could not use the book she was researching as her dissertation because by then it would be a published item by the time she completed her doctorate. Ravitch (1988) goes on to tell, that in light of that reality she contemplated different topics for her dissertation but had difficulty getting pass the idea that *The Great School War* should serve as her dissertation despite the objections. Ravitch even had the good fortune of being able to avoid the peer review aspect of her dissertation making it clear that she was unwilling to suffer other students picking apart her writing, and telling her what she had overlooked, and that after years of research she should go back and rewrite her work just on their say so. Being compelled by the minute criticism of her classmates to explore some obscure and unimportant notions was simply not something Ravitch was willing to submit herself to, and so she waged the war to resist having to endure that silly process. This tenacity, unrelenting persistence and refusal to take no for an answer is to be admired, but having the right connections does not hurt in a case like this. One has to think that Ravitch relates that story more to demonstrate what is possible within the system, particularly with those willing to pursue their goals aggressively. The story demonstrates the tremendous flexibility that lies within the system to make room for and to bend the rule for one who is absolutely certain of where they're going and their rights to that which they are after. In short, it may be said, that when the stars are properly aligned for the individual, what appears to be impossible is then made quite feasible. This inspiring personal story of Dianne Ravitch, and her research covering the public school system in New York City from its very beginning in the early nineteenth century, may be representative of the finest example of all that is right with education in the United States and perhaps the most telling fact that the system that is so talked over, has built within it the very solutions to its own maladies. Having documented the shortcomings of the New York City public school system, of the public school system in other states, and the shortcomings in the system of education in the United States as a whole, Ravitch is seen by many as one of the most prolific writers on that particular subject matter. However, given her own fast tract to academic success, one would think that Ravitch would have given some thought to the countless other very talented men and women in the United States who were deserving of a similar opportunity to make their contribution in improving the educational system. She would have been, and could still be the ideal person to carry out that search for talent and promote those who are more than qualified to assist in fixing this very fixable problem, a problem she herself has written so much about. One can venture to guess that the creative problem solvers that pioneered so much success in the private sector, particularly in the field of technology as well as other areas of business, has not had its equal in academia, and that this void represents an enormous opportunity for those willing to fill said void. Ravitch (1988) leaves us with the impression that the problems within the public school system in New York City and the public school system around the country are fixable, and that this is particularly so if the aggressive creative problem solving individuals were to be a part of the team conducting the repair. Ravitch (1988), argue that the public schools in every generation have had critics, crisis, and controversies, that the church state issue had not been solved by either centralization or decentralization, and that the education of poor children has consistently been the most vexing dilemma of the city's public school since 1805, adding that the public school must now educate virtually everyone, as they never did in the past, and they must educate themselves to a standard of literacy and numeracy that was never expected. In the past, important changes in society required changes in schooling. However, children today are subjected to extreme social stresses that were virtually unknown to previous generations. Examples of those risks are family dissolution, drugs, and crime (p. xviii). It might also be worth pointing out that up until the eighties the average PhD program for one who possessed a valid Master's degree was 36 credits to be completed in three years or less. Today with education becoming the giant shell game that it is, with hustlers and shysters from all parts of the business world getting in on the action, the average PhD for someone holding a valid master's is 90 credits, with some schools demanding as much as 140 to nearly 200 credits. The level of intellect within these classrooms is wanting. People openly discuss their personal lives, and bring to the table a level of reasoning that is hardly above that of a fifth grader. In short, it is pathetic. There is need for a new approach to education, one that will put these hustlers out of business and return sanity and intellect to what used to be referred to as graduate school.

There are countless individuals whose knowledge base and profession, qualifies them for the type of award Ravitch was able to secure for herself, and the creativity required for making this happen on a more massive scale is now at hand. It is the intention of this organization, the International Center for Intellectual Development, to bring about this reality. If such an organization exists we will not hesitate to join them, but in the absence of such a system, we will immediately go about the business of creating it. Why is this important? There are individuals around the world young and old, and of all races and backgrounds who are in need of help, in need of the kind of clarity that can greatly improve their lives. Providing this help requires a solid understanding of human history, and a good conceptualization of the human experience. I contend that there are a good number of men and women who fit that category, who simply has not had the opportunity to obtain the credits they deserve for the knowledge they have accumulated. We will fix that if it is the last thing we do. These individuals will immediately become the active problem solvers of our times, they will be the active thinkers and organizers armed with the wisdom and level headedness to correct a variety of socio-economic imbalances. The advisers and consultants under contract with the International Center for Intellectual Development have a simple approach to the issue of addiction; they empower addicts to do for themselves, by looking at those who have successfully worked their way out of addiction using the latest and most effective protocol. It is simple. For those hooked on stimulants: alcohol, cocaine and other drugs, they recommend the Ameisen protocol established by the famous French physician. For those hooked on heroin and other hard-core drugs they recommend the protocol established by Eric Taub and others who have had great results with the use of Ibogaine. That, in essence, is the extent of their recommendations to addicts, and it is done pretty much with a "take it or leave it" approach. That is because these professionals reserve much of their time to making sure children and young people are kept safe from the menace of addiction. Those addicts determined to continue going down their self-destructive path are free to do so undisputed by this organization and its mission.

I mention the case of Diane Ravitch because it is my firm belief that she can and will play a more significant role in improving the socio-economic situation in the United States of America. In the early sixties John Kennedy attempted to improve the world through the Alliance for Progress (Alianza para el Progreso). This dream was manifested through the Peace Corps where brave and idealistic young American were sent throughout the world to do what they can in making the world a better place. The program lost much of its impetus when that great American president was assassinated.

It is the goal of this author to create an alliance between forces such as the current secretary of education of the Obama administration Arnie Duncan, Dianne Ravitch, Ophra Winfrey and other well-meaning philanthropists, to create a condition through which more advanced thinkers in this country can pursue a fast tract PhD in the humanities, this with the explicit purpose of using that degree to raise the intellectual standards of the children of this country and the intellectual standards of the children of the world. It is my firm belief that when we raise the intellectual standards of children everywhere, everyone benefits. This includes children of all ages. That; I declare; is the goal I will be pursuing in the remaining years of my life. I ask that you join me in this pursuit.

*Combating Ignorance and Powerlessness*

## The History of Childhood

I begin this book with the history of childhood because I believe that for the purpose of effective communication it is imperative that we develop an understanding of the treatment we as a specie have meted out to children in nearly every region, and in just about every era including the present. This profound and most basic knowledge of ourselves is a necessary component of our collective self-analysis.

deMause (1974) declared that: "The history of childhood is a nightmare from which we have only recently began to awaken. The further back in history one goes, the lower the level of child care, and the more likely children are to be killed, abandoned, beaten, terrorized, and sexually abused" (p.1)

deMause's continuous reference to psychogenic reminds us of the possible relationship that may exist between our current socio-economic problems, and the treatment meted out to children for nearly all of human history, as each traumatized generation of children, acts out their repressed resentment and anger as adults. Because of the complexity of this statement I must turn once again to deMause for an accurate explanation. deMause explains this by arguing that the central force for change in our society is neither technology nor economics, but the psychogenic changes in personality occurring because of successive generations of parent child interactions. This argument is supported with five basic hypotheses:

1- The first of these hypotheses is that the evolution of parent child relationship constitutes an independent source of historical change. The origin of this evolution lies in the ability of successive generations of parents to regress to the psychic age of the children and work through the anxieties of that age in a better manner the second time they encounter them than they did during their own childhood, a process similar to that offered in psychoanalysis when the patient is offered a second chance at childhood through regression.

2- The second is that the generational pressure for psychic change is not only spontaneous, originating in the adult's need to regress and in the child's striving for relationship, but also occurs independent of the social and technological change. This allows it to be present even during periods of social and technological stagnation.

3- The third of these hypotheses presented by deMause states that the history of childhood is a series of closer approaches between adult and child, with each closing of psychic distance producing fresh anxiety, and that the aim of each generation is the reduction of these anxieties.

4- The fourth states simply that the further back we go in time the more evidence of abuse are revealed.

5- The last of these hypotheses presented by deMause states that because psychic structures must always be passed from generation to generation through the narrow funnel of childhood, a society's child rearing practices are not just one item in a list of cultural traits; they are the very condition for the transmission and development of all other cultural elements, and place definite limits on what can be achieved in all other spheres of history

(p. 3). These hypotheses presented by deMause may not have answered all the questions regarding unresolved childhood issues and their surfacing in adulthood, but they do amplify the subject and help us to understand its complex nature.

deMause also introduce us to Phillip Aries, another writer who dedicated much of his time and energy to the subject of childhood history, and one who was also researched extensively for this report. Aries wrote and published *Centuries of Childhood* in 1962 one of the books most credited on this subject. Aries (1962), states that medieval art until about the twelfth century did not know childhood or did not attempt to portray it. It is hard to believe that this neglect was due to incompetence or incapacity; it seems more probable that there was no place for childhood in the medieval world (p. 33). Aries (1962) does not claim there were no young people, what there was rather, was an abundance of young humans between the ages of 7 and 15. These however, were not seen as children, since the culture of the time lacked the concept of childhood. In the medieval world a young person of 7 was already an adult, and particularly in their attire, there was hardly anything to distinguish the child from the adult (p.50). Aries added that most young people were apprenticed, became workers in the fields (later, after the industrial revolution, in the factories) and generally entered fully into the adult society at a very early age (p. 37). As evidence of the absence of the child figure Aries cites the art work of the period, most of which has survived to our times. He points out that there is a glaring absence of children. Babies are present, but children as we know them, are nowhere to be found. What we find are little adults. The musculature, dress, expressions, and mannerisms are all adult like. It is said that some art historians have attempted to explain this phenomenon away suggesting that the artists lacked the skill to paint children. Aries suggests another explanation, the one generally accepted today, namely that they couldn't paint young people as children because they were not children. In their cultures they were little adults, and this is precisely what the artists' saw (p.56).

According to deMause (1974), the central thesis of *Centuries of Childhood* is that children were happier in that they were free to mix with many classes and ages, but that a special condition known as childhood was invented in the early modern period, resulting in a tyrannical concept of the family which destroyed friendship and sociability and deprived children of freedom, inflicting on them for the first time the birch and the prison cell, and according to deMause (1974) Aries uses two main arguments to prove that point: The first is that a separate concept of childhood was unknown in the early Middle Ages. The second argument is that the modern family restricts the child's freedom and increases the severity of punishment. In deMause's opinion, this argument runs contrary to all the evidence available to us regarding children in antiquity, that Aries ignores the voluminous evidence that medieval artists could, indeed, paint realistic children. To conclude his criticism of Aries, deMause refers to his notion of a separate concept of childhood being unknown, as an untenable idea, and he refers to the notion of the invention of childhood as, fuzzy (pp. 5-6).

We learned from Aries that once the institution of childhood began to emerge, the situation of the young person began to

change in society as we find in Aries (1962), "About the thirteenth century, a few types of children are to be found which
appear to be a little closer to the modern concept of childhood"
(p. 34).

Even though Aries was not a sociologist it is hard to imagine anyone writing extensively about the history of childhood
and not include the widespread incidences of abuse that had already come to the attention of those who cared enough to know.
Those reports came to us through writers like George Payne, G.
Rattray Taylor, and Luis Despert daring enough to take on those
issues. deMause (1974), briefly describes the works of each of
these writers, commenting on George Henry Payne that he was
the first to examine the wide extent of infanticide and brutality
towards children (p.6). George Henry Payne was an author of
the late nineteenth and early twentieth century who maintained
a close friendship with the noted Dr. Abraham Jacobi, the
German American physician who pioneered Pediatric care in
New York and the rest of the United States. Payne was noted
for two publications: *The Child in Human History* (1916) and
*The History of Journalism in the United States* (1920). The forward to *The Child in Human History* was written by Jacobi who
stated among other things that, "Without the history of the child
there can be no scientific knowledge of the thousands of years
of child life. Nobody has given it a second thought, until the
author of this book offered us the wealth of his vast studies" (p.
v). Other than DeMause and Jacobi, this research has found
hardly any comments regarding George Payne and his work.
deMause (1974), then describes Gordon Rattray Taylor's (1973)
publication *The Angel Maker*, as a sophisticated psychoanalytic

reading of childhood and personality in late eighteenth-century England. deMause then describes David Hunt's (1970) publication as being parallel to that of Aries, as it too centers mostly on the unique seventeen century document, Heroard's diary of the childhood of Luis the XIII, but does so with great sensitivity and awareness of the psycho historical implications of his findings. Finally, deMause (1974) refers to Louise Despert's (1965) as a psychiatric comparison of child mistreatment in the past and present, one that surveys the range of emotional attitudes towards children since antiquity, expressing her growing horror as she uncovers a story of unremitting heartlessness and cruelty (p.6).

In an essay appearing in the (1992) publication of The *Journal of Psychohistory 25.* (3), deMause stated:

> My conclusions from a lifetime of psycho historical study of childhood and society, is that the history of humanity is founded upon the abuse of children. Just as family therapist today find that child abuse often functions to hold families together as a way of solving their emotional problems, so too, the routine assault of children has been society's most effective way of maintaining its collective emotional homeostasis (p.1).

To this deMause (1974) adds the charge that most historical families once practiced infanticide, incest, and beating and mutilation of their children to relieve anxieties (p.97), and later in the nineteenth century Luis Adamic described being brought up in an Eastern European village of "killing nurses" where mothers sent their infants to be done away with " by exposing them to cold air after a hot bath; feeding them with something that causes convulsion in their stomach and intestines; mixing gyp-sum in their milk, which literally plastered up their insides; suddenly stuffing them with food after not giving them anything to eat for two days…"(p. 29). deMause (1974) adds that Adam-ic was to have been killed as well, but for some reason his nurse spared him. Adamic's account of how he watched her do away with the other babies she received provides a picture of the emotional reality behind all those centuries of infanticide we have been reviewing (p. 29).

deMause (1974), also disputes the allegations that infanti-cide is an Eastern rather than a Western problem, arguing that infanticide of both legitimate and illegitimate children was a regular practice of antiquity, one in which many nations and ethnic groups participated. The practice was largely played down; he goes on to say; despite the hundreds of references by the ancients that it was an accepted, everyday occurrence. Chil-dren were thrown into rivers, flung into dung heaps, cesspools and trenches, potted in jars to starve to death, and exposed on every hill and roadside, a prey for birds, and food for wild beast to rend. There were gynecological writings at the time instruct-ing parents on how to recognize a child that is worth rearing and any child that did not fit this description was killed (p. 29). de Mause commented that a first born was invariably kept alive but only if they were healthy, this was so, particularly if they were boys. (p.26) Girls ran a gloomier fate, as described in a letter of a man by the name of Hilarion; who was away from home; to his pregnant wife Alis (1 B.C.): "If, as may well happen, you give birth to a child, if it's a boy let it live; if it's a girl, expose it" (p.26). One would be inclined to conclude, given this sce-

nario that the sex ratio would be greatly upset, but deMause re-
futes that too on the basis that boys and girls of illegitimate
birth, were killed equally. What is even more baffling is deM-
ause's statement that legitimate children of wealthy parents
were also killed regularly; so much so that the historian Polybi-
us felt the need to point out how much the practice had affected
the Greek population.

Not only was the killing of children a common practice
throughout Europe and other parts of the world, there were no
laws on the books banning the horrendous practice. deMause
(1974) gives us the words of the celebrated Greek philosopher
Aristotle regarding this:"As to exposing or rearing the children
born, let there be a law that no deformed child shall be reared."
(p.26). deMause (1974) also shared with us the opinion of Ar-
istipus, another celebrated Greek philosopher and pupil of Soc-
rates, who was even more gruesome in his description of children and the treatment they deserved:

> ...a man could do what he wants with his children, for,
> do we not cast away from ourselves our spittle, lice and
> such like, as things unprofitable, which nevertheless are
> engendered and bread even out of our own selves...Mad
> dogs we knock on the head; the fierce and savage ox we
> slay; sickly sheep we put to the knife to keep them from
> infecting the flock; unnatural progeny we destroy; we
> drown even children who at birth are weakly and ab-
> normal. Yet it is not anger, but reason that separates the
> harmful from the sound. (p.27)

deMause (1974) explains that the European's process of
murdering their children was a calm, deliberate and well

thought out one, despite the horror and brutality it represents. He refers to thousands of bones dug up in various archeological sites with many inscriptions defining the victims as first born, findings going back as early as 7,000 B.C (p.27). He tells us of children being sealed in walls, and in foundations of buildings and bridges in order to strengthen their structure; a practice that was common from the building of the wall of Jericho to as late as 1843 in Germany. Whenever new ventures were begun, children would be sacrificed. Whenever a new building or bridge was built, a child would be buried within it as a foundation sacrifice. He refers to the game many of us knew as children *London Bridge is Falling Down,* as the acting out a sacrifice to a river goddess (p.27). Whether he is referring to those who were sacrificed in her waters or those that were used to strengthen the bridge structure is hard to say, but the symbolism is undoubtedly effective.

In attempting to assess the rate of infanticide in the Middle Ages, deMause (1974) makes reference to Innocente III who opened the hospital de Santo Spirito in Rome at the end of the twelfth century, adding that he was aware of the number of women throwing their babies into the Tiber. He also added that as late as 1527, one priest admitted that "the latrines resound with the cries of children who have been plunged into them." (p.29)

Infanticide may have meant different things to different people over time, across culture and in various societies and it is difficult to embark on this subject without becoming judgmental. For some the practice cannot be either understood or justified.

9

This is not an attempt to analyze infanticide as a phenomenon, it is simply too deep and too horrifying for any form of analysis. Uncovering the phenomenon, reporting on it and developing some understanding of its nature is enough of a challenge. The absence of professionals, either in the sociological or in the psychological field daring to take on this subject is also intriguing. One can hardly read deMause's work without becoming ill physically or emotionally, for the revelations defy all sense of decency and humanity. Any effort to analyze the practice runs the risk of explaining it away or making excuses for it. My personal interest is relegated to the intrapsychic reality of those responsible for such acts over such extended period.

Viviana Zelizer (1985) *Pricing the Priceless Child* is in essence a study of the Life Insurance market and how this market affected the life of children in one period in American life. Zelizer attempts to explain in her book how monetary interest intersects with sacred concerns, including a focus on what she refers to as the economically worthless but emotionally priceless child in the United States between 1870 and 1930. In her study Zelizer examines three major institutions that are directly involved in the valuation of a child's life, namely: children's insurance, the sale and adoption of children and the changing value of the child during that period.

Like Aries before her, Zelizer completely avoids the issue of child abuse or infanticide revealed by writers like deMause, Alice Miller and Murray Strauss. It could be said that Zelizer's books deals primarily with the issue of life insurance for children since the few cases of abuse or murder that she alludes to are all connected to the value of the child as this new insurable commodity (p.152). In fact the term insurance appears on 74 separate pages of Zelizer's book, while child abuse is mentioned on only four of the pages within the text. Child murder is mentioned on seven occasions and the only time infanticide is mentioned was to refer the reader to another writer on the subject of childhood history.

Zelizer explains that with drastic changes in the laws governing child labor turn-of-the-century America was lead into discovering new, sentimental criteria to determine a child's monetary worth. The heightened emotional status of children resulted, for example, in the legal justification of children's life insurance policies and in large damages awarded by courts to their parents in the event of death. It denotes the shift from late 19th century views of children as wage earners, to the modern view of children as a sacred entity. The first chapter looks at the startling change in response to child death. Once considered a detached loss of economic contribution, child death becomes cause for emotional outbursts of grief and loss. As an eye-opening example, Zelizer cites two scenarios in which a child is killed by a street car, and the child's parents go before the courts for restitution. In the first case, occurring in the late 19th century, the parents are told that because the child was not old enough to provide for the family, he was thus economically useless, and the courts could not award any damages for his death. Zelizer contrasts this with a similar case in the early 20th century, where the court found that while a sum of money could ease suffering, no amount of money could replace the loss of a child. By then, the attitude towards children and their value had undergone considerable changes.

Zelizer (1985) points to Aries comment that the "early surge of sensitivity toward the value of children's lives in Europe, preceded by more than a century any reduction in mortality. The first portraits of dead children proving that the child was no longer...considered an inevitable loss, appeared as early as the sixteenth century, a period of demographic wastage" (31).

Zelizer (1985) then introduces Harvard PhD. Graduate Edward Shorter's (1976), *The Making of the Modern Family* in which Shorter offers an alternative to the rational investment hypothesis:

> After showing that the surge for sentiment for children in Europe preceded any reduction in mortality rates, Shorter argues that the shift from traditional indifference to greater concern for children was itself responsible for improving longevity. According to the better love hypothesis, maternal concern for child life and death actively shaped demographic patterns. Traditional mothers, argues Shorter, did not care, and that is why their children vanished in the ghastly slaughter of the innocent that was traditional child rearing. As soon as mothers learned to love properly, child mortality plunged (p.31).

Zelizer goes beyond the changes in the economic value of children, to venture into a more in-depth analysis of the new reaction to child death. Her case was centered on the concept of the play-ground versus street-play, and the consequences of street playing in the new age of the automobile. We find in Zelizer (1985) that:

Between 1910 and 1913, over 40 percent of New York traffic victims were under fifteen years of age. In 1914, the rate jumped to 60 percent, with a high rate of fatalities, especially among those between the ages of five and ten. Death from street accidents were nearly three times as many as any single disease, and Zelizer tells us that most of those accidents took place within a block or two from the child's home, while the child play or ran an errand for his or her parents. Being a child, concluded one observer, and had become *the most dangerous job in the world* (p.35).

Zelizer (1985) tell us that the sight of children grounded up under street cars was very common (p.37). But by the late twenties the attitude towards such deaths had changed. A child's death under these circumstances began to generate public acts of outrage, with neighborhood mobs spontaneously demonstrating their solidarity with the grief of bereaved parents by fiercely attacking those who they referred to as the killers of children. Memorial acts of remembrance became commonplace, and prevention campaigns as well as education about child safety and health was in full force (27).

By showing the concern for child safety across class, Zelizer effectively argues that changes in attitudes around childhood encompassed more than just economic factors. The creation of mothering programs, public health initiatives, preschools, playgrounds, and child spaces were efforts that both reduced risk to children, and increased the assimilation of low-class immigrant children, including a study of the difference in attitude and perception between poor and rich children.

In the second half of the book, Zelizer looks to profound changes in the life insurance industry, tort law, and adoption/foster care resulting from the changed value of children. Created from the conception of child worth, the notion of child insurance became a scandalous effort to commercialize the life of a child, and later morphed to become an acceptable form of funding for the possible funeral of a working-class child. Thus, insurance became a symbolic recognition of the value of a child, even a poor child, and insuring children became a common and profitable business.

The core question, as Zelizer (1985) states it, is how to "assess value when price is absent." The great paradox is that the assigned value of a child increased, while the actual economic value (as a child laborer) decreased. A child's value upon death now became a function of their sentimental, rather than economic value (14).

As another demonstration of the dramatic shift in perception of child worth, Zelizer explains the late 1900's trend of mothers paying to get rid of children through baby farms, to the new high-priced industry of buying infants for adoption. As opposed to wanting children for economic gain, Zelizer analyzes how "adoption practices were revolutionized into a search for child love and not child labor" (p.170). Earlier adoption and foster care practices were used as a "quasi-employment" for families, and often poor women would abandon their babies for lack of anyone that wanted them. Zelizer (1985) convincingly argues that the efforts of child welfare workers, taking advantage of the sentimentalization of childhood, worked to reform adoption and foster parenting into culturally popular prac-

14

tice. "The quest for a child to love turned into a glamorous and romanticized search as a number of well-known entertainment and political figures proudly and publicly joined the rank of adoptive parents" (p. 190).

As our society struggles with its current level of anger and senseless violence, it behooves us to explore the past for some answers to this complex and troubling conundrum. This research paper is a minor contribution to what has to be a future gargantuan effort that must be undertaken if we are to quell the insanity and the wanton violence that is now commonplace in this and in so many other societies around the globe. Our continuous failure to span backwards in earnest and honesty can only produce more of what Despert (1970) refers to as the emotional cripples, many of whom occupy positions of power and prominence affecting the lives of far too many of their fellow human beings. This is not to say that the violence today is worse than in any previous period in history, after all nothing has stop the unspeakable carnage of the two world wars and the various civil wars preceding them. What makes our era so special is that never before have we been so equipped as a species to study this behavior, and even though the subject of child maltreatment has been largely absent from academic work, this very void creates a promising future for this area of study as it is so desperately needed, after all every generation must find or produce the answers to its own predicaments, and most of these answers are locked up in the past. The challenge of course is in the coordination of this undertaking since it appears no academic field is willing to tackle this subject on its own. We have seen where psychologists, starting with Sigmund Freud had difficulty accepting the reports of parental abuse in his native Austria, and as deMause (2002) reports, most historians have assiduously avoided psychology, either saying that history consists in saying what happened, more, or trying to explain history by impersonal structural forces, as though such a passionate human enterprise as history could be impersonal" (p. 88). deMause (2002) further argues that genocide may be seen as one of the worst forms of human cruelty but even there, historians appear to avoid the psychodynamics of the perpetrators of war leaving it up to the psychologists (p. 138). deMause (2002) further argues that the concern is not for how the perpetrator got the weapon but for the internal development of the perpetrator's psyche and his or her opportunity to carry out the act (p. 139). deMause (2002) then offers the opinion of a prison psychiatrist James Gilligan on this subject. Gilligan had spent his life analyzing the lives of criminals and his opinion was that: some people think armed robbers commit crimes in order to get money. But when you sit down and talk with people who repeatedly commit such crimes, what you hear is, I never got so much respect before in my life as I did when I first pointed a gun at somebody (p. 139).

Gilligan's analysis sums up most of what this report is intended to convey, that disrespect for the child produces hostility among a host of other emotions and that only when society as a whole recognizes this and realizes the importance of treating children with the deserved respect, will we begin to address this most vexing problem.

The callousness and brutality of the Sicilian mafia has long been of concern to many, wondering what human circumstances could have produced that level of depravity. deMause (2002) may well have found the answer in researching the work of the Italian psychoanalyst Silvia diLorenzo. In the book La Grande Madre Mafia diLorenzo describes actual Sicilian mother child interactions and offers her version of the maternal origins of Mafia violence:

If a boy of theirs commits a slight fault, [mothers] do not resort to simple blows, but they pursue him on a public street and bite him on the face, the ears, and the arms until they draw blood. In those moments even a beautiful woman is transformed in physiognomy, she become purplish-red, with blood-shot eyes, with gnashing teeth, and trembling convulsions, and only the hastening of others, who with difficulty tear away the victim, put an end to such savage scenes (p. 153). The source of that mother's rage and anger is an altogether different subject.

## VIOLENCE TO CHILDREN IN OUR TIMES

After exploring some of the psychological reasons for parents' violence on children, this chapter will deal with the mechanism that allows some parents to reject the long standing custom of disciplining their children by way of violence. Intended to be an active, functional document, the research will explore the persuasive language and instruments to be used in creating some ambivalence in those parents and other adults that steadfastly stand by the old customs of submitting children to adult's violence.

The epidemic of violence sweeping the world today has succeeded in tearing apart families and communities, stretching the resources of many social service agencies to its limits. This epidemic has also rendered vast sections of many countries around the world off limits and un-inhabitable to anyone with civilized behavior. Interestingly enough, this is not the first generation of humans grappling with wholesale gratuitous violence. Since the invention of weapons, humans have created extraordinary and sophisticated ways of hurting each other, a behavior that leads to many armed conflicts, and that is also intensified during the course of these conflicts. This wholesale violence took on new dimension with the invention of gunpowder, a product that became synonymous with facilitating killing. Repeated statements that weapons are not the cause of violence may have numbed our senses to these issues of violence and may have also reduced the responsibility we each have for studying this phenomenon, defining its cause and eventually bringing it under control.

The first question that is asked in this report is whether violence is just a by-product of the irresistible desire the strong has for taking advantage of the weak when the opportunity presents itself? Would this then be a confirmation of the violent nature of the species and that violence may be coded in our DNA?

The answers to these questions may never be found, but their absence behooves those of us who care about the future of the species to come together in the search for, or the formulation of.

Sigmund Freud, the celebrated father of psychology and psychoanalysis, dedicated little or non of his time or energy to the study of the cause of violence in humans, despite the fact that a massive war; and the horrible cruelty leading up to another; took place in his lifetime. Even with two world wars behind us, the species failed to produce an industry designed to steadily and consistently analyze the cause of violence in humans. Not until recently did it begin to dawn on a few psychologists that the cause of violence may be deeply rooted in childhood, that this strong desire to feel superior to other human beings may be really the cause of nearly all the misery we've heaped on each other since the dawn of civilization. The idea that these concepts are generated in us in our childhood years should be enough to give pause and take stock at the way we treat those human beings whose care we have been entrusted with.

This book is expected to be a significant part of the on-going discussion on the subject of violence towards children as it implores the energy and engagement of everyone who shares the dream of a future world free of violence, convinced that the sacred concept of non-violence towards children begins in the home with the child. Non-violence in words, non-violence in deeds, and non-violence in actions.

The most unfortunate thing with the issue of the psychological reasons for violence towards children is that so few resources are available on the subject; it is almost as if writers and researchers have purposely stayed away from this extremely sensitive subject. Yet, it is the argument of so many that without willingness for open dialogue on the subject, the reality of our daily lives as it relates to violence, has reduced chances of ever improving.

Radda Barnen the Swedish version of *Save the Children* issued a pamphlet entitled *Hitting People Is Wrong - and Children Are People Too*. The pamphlet was later published by EPOCH (End Physical Punishment of Children) an informal alliance of organizations, which share the aim of ending all physical punishment of children by education and legal reform. The pamphlet is a list of six answers describing why parents hit children and in the final of these answers it states: "Many parents are under stress from difficult socio-economic conditions. Forbidding physical punishment would add to that stress and should await better standards of living." The pamphlet goes on to say—"This argument is a tacit admission of an obvious truth: physical punishment is often an outlet for the pent-up feelings of adults rather than an attempt to educate children" (p.1).

The article goes on to argue that in most parts of the world parents urgently need more social and economic support than they get, but they refuse to accept this behavior as justifications for venting their frustrations on children. They assert that children's protection from physical punishment must not be dependent on improvements in the socio-economic arrangements in their parents' lives. What is worse, they argue, hitting children is seldom an effective stress-reliever and cite as evident that most parents who hit out in temper experience guilt and wish that they could find other ways of disciplining their children.

The argument made by the pamphlet is that alternatives to physical punishments are not different punishments but an approach to 'discipline' which is positive rather than punitive, and they cite research showing that effective control of children's behavior does not depend upon punishment for wrong-doing but on clear and consistent limits that prevent it. They explain that adults modeling and an explanation of the behavior they would prefer for the child seems

21

to have a more positive effect on curbing the child's behavior (p.2).

A more radical approach to this subject was offered by Jordan Riak head of the Parents and Teachers Against Violence. In the 1992 issue of the organization's newsletter Riak published an essay entitled Plain Talk About Spanking and in the essay Riak argues that many spankers are habituated to the practice because it provides them with an instant outlet for their feelings of frustration and anger - not because they've found it an effective way to improve a child's behavior. The danger of this he argues, is that violence, by its very nature, tend to escalate as it is indulged in, thus making it impossible for there to be a safe way to hit a child (p.1).

Riak (1992), then goes on to make the connection between spanking and sexual molestation telling us that spanked children learn that their bodies are not their personal property, and that allowing someone else to do as they please with their bodies opens the gate for that someone or others to do the same or even more, and that even their sexual areas are subject to the will of adults. The child who submits to a spanking on Monday is not likely to say no to a molester on Tuesday. So no matter what else violent parents think they are accomplishing with their behavior, they are setting children up to be easy prey for predators (p.2).

The other area in which those parents try to justify their behavior is arguing that the buttocks is safe because of its meaty structure but Riak then commented that medical science has long recognized and documented in great detail how being struck on the buttocks can stimulate sexual feelings. Riak (1992), makes it clear that located deep in the buttocks is the sciatic nerve, the largest nerve in the body and that a severe blow to the buttocks, particularly with a blunt instrument, could cause bleeding in the muscles that surround that nerve, possibly injuring it and causing impairment to the involved leg. Riak (1992), adds that a blow to the buttocks can cause injury to the tailbone (coccyx) or sacrum. It sends force waves upward through the spinal column possibly causing disc compression or compression fractures of vertebral bones. And as far as the old claim that God or nature intended that part of the anatomy for spanking Riak argues that that claim is brazenly perverse since no part of the human body was made to be mistreated (p.4).

The tragic consequence for many children who have been punished by spanking, according to Riak (1992), is that they form a connection between pain, humiliation and sexual arousal that endures for the rest of their lives. Riak then proceeds to introduce David Bakan, author of *Slaughter of the Innocents*, in which Bakan wrote:

"...The buttocks are the locus for the induction of pain in a child. We are familiar with the argument that it is a safe

23

'locus' for spanking. However, the anal region is also the major erotic region at precisely the time the child is likely to be beaten there. Thus it is aptly chosen to achieve the result of deranged sexuality in adulthood..." (Bakan 1971, p. 113). Riak (1992), continues to present the argument for no-spanking telling us that the pornography and prostitution industries do a thriving business catering to the needs of countless unfortunate individuals whose sexual development has been derailed by childhood spankings. If we put all other considerations aside, this should be reason enough never to spank a child (p.5).

The excuse that so many schools give that the hands are safe for hitting is also refuted by Riak (1992), stating that his research has revealed that the child's hand is particularly vulnerable because its ligaments, nerves, tendons and blood vessels are close to the skin, which has no underlying protective tissue. Striking the hands of younger children is especially dangerous to the growth plates in the bones, which, if damaged, can cause deformity or impaired function. Striking a child's hand can also cause fractures, dislocations and can lead to premature osteoarthritis, he argues. Many of us have also become familiar with the shaking baby syndrome, but not everyone has. Shaking a baby that is crying annoyingly seems innocuous to many uninformed parents specially those parents in the lower strata of our society, and those in the developing world, so the damage or death to those children will forever go unde-tected (p.5).

Riak (1992), ends his comments by telling us that we should not be surprised that many youngsters reject the adult world to the degree they believe it has rejected them. Nor should we be surprised that those who throughout childhood have been recipients of violence will become dispensers of it as soon as they are able. Some teachers work tirelessly to curb violence-impacted children's ag-gressiveness, to instill trust which those children lack, and to redirect their energies in positive directions but that is a daunting task even for the most dedicated and best pre-pared teachers since it requires extraordinary resources currently inaccessible to the current public school systems. School dropout, addiction and delinquency would cease to be major problems if only it were possible to persuade par-ents and other caretakers to stop socializing children in ways likely to make them antisocial and/or self-destructive (p. 6).

## The Victor Frankl Experience

Fitting the Victor Frankl experience in this chapter is quite a stretch as the reader may ask what it has to do with the subject of violence to children. They'll soon realize however, that the story of man's inhumanity to man is one that repeats itself throughout human history. This survivor of the Nazi death camp tells a compelling story in great detail, and with a deeply philosophical approach adding tremendously to the vast knowledge already compiled about these death camps and the horrors within.

The essay focused on Frankl's willingness or ability to concentrate on the sublime and powerful nature of his love for his wife as his source of strength for surviving the horrors of the concentration camp. The magic of the experience is highlighted when Frankl (1992), shared:

> I did not know whether my wife was alive, and I had no means of finding out...[but] there was no need for me to know, nothing could touch the strength of my love, my thoughts and the image of my beloved. Had I known that my wife was dead, I think that I would still have given myself, undisturbed by that knowledge, to the contemplation of her image and that my mental conversations with her would have been just as vivid and just as satisfying (p50).

The above quote describes an extraordinary mechanism for coping with suffering, one not unlike that developed by children in captivity experiencing unimaginable horrors at the hands of some adults, horrors that often stretches out for multiple years, which to all would seem like an eternity. Frankl's actions were conscious and were aided by his lifetime experience as an adult, children in the hands of abusing adults have no such luxury, their coping mechanisms must be created out of thin air, and pure imagination.

The unfortunate thing about the Frankl experience and that of the entire holocaust is that we learned very little from it, human slaughter went on unabated almost immediately after the Nazi camps were closed. Ardrey (1963), tells us that the roots of human ancestry is steeped in violence, and he does so by quoting the South African anthropologist Raymond Dart's 1953 paper entitled *The Predatory Transition from Ape to Man* in making his case. Dart's study lead him to the conclusion that man's ancestors were killer apes and that their weapons of choice in those early days had been the antelope humerus bone. Ardrey (1963), tells us that what Dart put forward in his piece was the simple thesis that Man had emerged from the anthropoid background for one reason only, and that is because he was a killer. Ardrey goes on to quote Dart as saying:

> Long ago, perhaps many millions of years ago, a line of killer apes branched off from the non-aggressive primate background. For reasons of environmental necessity, the line adopted the predatory way. For reasons of predatory necessity the line advanced. We learned to stand erect in the first place as a necessity of hunting life. We learned to run in our pursuit of game across the yellowing African savannah. Our hands freed from the mauling and the hauling, we had no further use for a snout; and so it

retreated. And lacking fighting teeth and claws, we took recourse by necessity to the weapon (p. 29).

Through Ardrey (1963), Raymond Dart goes on to present his case that this weapon could be a rock, a stick or a heavy bone and that in either of these cases it would have meant the margin of survival for our ancestral killer, but he added that the use of the weapon represented new and multiplying demands on the nervous system for the coordination of muscle, touch and sight. This combination of factors, argued Dart, contributed to the creation of a larger brain, a necessary requirement for modern man. Since that period, argued Dart, Man has become a slave to the weapon, in other words, the weapon had fathered man (p.29). Dart's theory reflects significantly on the horrors on Nazi Germany despite the fact that it avoids the concept of the mistreatment of children as a contributing factor to the horrors we've all become so familiar with.

Ardrey (1963) does not answer the question of whether violence is imprinted in the species' DNA but the hypothesis regarding the weapon comes close to making that particular point. If Dart is right and violence has been with the species since its genesis, then it may well be that only through emotional and intellectual growth taking place at a massive level, that we will be able to overcome our violent tendencies. One perfect place to begin however is with the children, perhaps a massive campaign encouraging parents

and caretakers to resist the urge to use violence with promises of reward to those who succeed in this effort.

## POST TRAUMATIC SLAVERY DISORDER

The system that allows some human beings to own other human beings can be traced back to the earliest civilizations, proof of this are the endless conversations and accusations held today regarding the captivity of Jews in Egypt and their role in the building of the pyramids. We also hear of slavery in connection to nearly every ethnic and racial group inhabiting the planet today so as we speak of the post traumatic slavery disorder it becomes necessary to identify the specific group to whom we are referring. Here again we're forced to revisit the issue of the weapon and how it has influenced the workings of our society.

In his *Destruction of Black Civilization: Great Issues of a Race*, published in 1987 by Third World Press African American historian Chancellor Williams speaks of the significance of gunpowder in the creation of that phenomenon we have come to know as the middle passage, a process that reduced an entire ethnic group to the status of slaves. Williams (1987), argues that this last government sanctioned form of slavery known to the specie would not have been possible if not for the invention and introduction of gunpowder in the form of weapons. In their contact with the Caucasians, the purpose of African chiefs was to obtain as many of these weapons as possible allowing them to expand their territories over weaker states eventually utilizing parts of their populations as slaves. The practice of utiliz-

30

ing conquered people as slaves or servants was widespread in the ancient world and prevalent on the African continent, so during the early stages of the slave trade many African chiefs and kings actually thought they were supplying workers needed abroad and in this case rather than keeping the slaves for themselves they would sell them to the Caucasians at a handsome profit (p.252).

Despite debates regarding its authenticity, the Willie Lynch document is one that has been discussed among Black students for quite some time. The authenticity of the document is immaterial given the fact that everything it relates to is part of the vivid slave experience, whether in the United States or in the Caribbean. The value of the document is that it helps scholars in developing some understanding of the roots of the complexities of self-hate among the ex-slaves, as well as other syndromes that are part of the daily conversations among Blacks but that they never quite gain full understanding of.

The document itself describes a complex mechanism the like of which we know was in fact used for breaking the will of the slaves and setting the slaves against each other for many generations. The story of the horrors of those five centuries of captivity must be left up to the human imagination since it is clear that only a tiny part of the story has really been told, so between the Lynch fable, our imagination and some of the real stories told so far, we arrive at some of the reasons for what is today referred to as the post traumatic slavery disorder, one characterized by the ex-slaves doing everything in their power to self destroy socially, politically, psychologically and physically.

Harvard psychiatrist Dr. Alvin Poussant offers an entirely different approach in the analysis of violence. Poussant (2000), argues that the glamorization of America's historic culture of violence must remain a central part of any discussion on the subject in our time, proceeding then to quote Walter Mosley's observation in *Working on the Chain Gang: Shaking off the Dead Hand of History*, Blacks in America have been, and continue to be, a petri dish of the nation's psychological health. Poussant (2000) insists that in analyzing the problems experienced by Blacks in the United States they must first be looked at as the symptom of a much larger and more deadly illness which is that America's social fabric has been woven through with violence. We gather from Poussant (2000) that it would be unfair for anyone to attempt to analyze the dysfunctionality and the psychopathologies of the African American without first endeavoring to understand the larger context from which it is derived (p. 87).

In arguing the post traumatic slavery disorder, Poussant (2000) states that African Americans have suffered formidable mental stresses that have been in part the manifestation of the legacy of slavery, which encompasses the twin burden of poverty and racism. Poussant goes on to tell us that the impact of racism by itself, independent of poverty, still appears to exact a toll on the minds and bodies of the descendants of the men and women brought to this continent as slaves, straining their capacity to adapt successfully in America. Researchers believe that racism has contributed to the high rates of hypertension, heart disease, and other stress-related illnesses in the black community. The perpetual status of second class citizenry is not a condition that all can cope with, so the escape by way of drugs, alcohol, depression or anti-social behavior is the unfortunate avenue for those who failed to cope (p.142).

## RADICAL NON-VIOLENCE, A PARADIGM SHIFT

Real non-violence represents a paradigm shift in the ways that human beings relate to each other. In this case it may also be referred to as radical non-violence because of its focus on the root causes of the anger and vitriol that seems to characterize human interactions.

Humanity has had three renowned non-violent advocates: the Palestinian Jesus Christ, the Hindu Mahatma Gandhi and African American Martin Luther King, and it is likely that there be a great many others dedicated to the cause of non-violence who we simply did not become aware of. In none of these three cases however, was there recognition of the damaging effects of the violence perpetrated against children in the name of discipline, none of these ambassadors of peace made a connection between violence to children and the violence of those same human beings after becoming adults. In his 1974 publication The History of Childhood Lloyd deMause reminds us that at the time of Jesus' birth, infanticide was a common practice throughout the world, including the Middle East and that his brief presence on this planet had no effect on this horrifying practice. deMause (1974) reminds us that sealing children in the walls and foundations of bridges and buildings to strengthen the structure was also common. From the building of the wall of Jericho to as late as 1843 in Germany (p.27). Likewise, we find none of Gandhi's writings reflects a specific interest in the safety and protection of children, the same is true for the writings issued by and about Martin Luther King. That is why this book argues that this new approach to non-violence is unprecedented, it pulls together all the forces in the community that may even remotely connect to children and brings them into the understanding that it behooves everyone to treat children with concern, love, and compassion.

It is the responsibility of every legitimate government to guarantee the safety and security of all of its citizens, particularly the most vulnerable. Fortunately, state and local governments around the world have been responding to the United Nations 1978 Declaration of the Right of the Child which says in essence that all children deserve to live in safety and security.

If the goal is non-violence in the home, particularly with respect to children, then government has within its power the ability to provide incentives for parents who sign on to an agreement to make every effort to reject violence in raising their children. Tax breaks, food surplus programs, high school diplomas or college credits for those who successfully comply are but a few of the options that with some creativity, government can make available to these parents and caretakers who have done their part in helping to create better citizens. However, this will not happen by itself, with this priority in mind, future organizers will learn to bring pressure to bear on both elected and appointed officials at all level of government to endorse these creative ideas whose ultimate effect will drastically reduce social problems and create a more functional citizenry.

Partnering with parents is essential to providing greater security for children, but for those parents who are already borderline dysfunctional or those whose method of discipline is deeply engrained, it will require a great deal of persuasion to convince them of the benefits of a new approach to raising their children. Children who have been raised successfully without corporal punishment may be the ambassadors for engaging other parents in an effort to persuade them as to the benefits of this non-violent approach to child rearing, for if parents become convinced that their children can do as well without the use of violence there is a chance they will consider this method particularly when the by-product of this new method is in their presence. Many of the parents who need to be dissuaded from the old methods are themselves functionally illiterate, so volumes of written materials may not be useful in this case, it will require a core of committed organizers that includes adolescents, concerned mothers, seniors and anyone else with the ability to persuade, to reach out to these parents and caretakers and convince them as to the validity of this new method.

The concluding thought in this chapter is that only a major, well-structured campaign against violence can really begin to force parents and other caregivers to take a second look at their behavior and contemplate other avenues for raising their children, and that is precisely what this book is expecting to generate. The power of persuasion must come to force in getting parents and other caretakers to understand that the issue at hand is the society at large and not just the child. Only then, will they realize that there is a certain connection between their current fears of walking the street at certain hours or of going into certain neighborhoods, and the practice of violence towards children. That connection is crucial to persuading the entire specie that it can in fact exist without violence, that violence is but a holdover from our troglodyte Neanderthal era, one in which violence was the most effective form of communication since speech, as we know it, had not yet been developed. The campaign must be effective in tying in non-violence against children with the worldwide campaign for non-violence among the people of the world. That campaign has significantly reduced the number of conflicts around the world; this new campaign will go a long way to reduce childhood trauma and childhood suffering. Its organizers and foot soldiers need to be clear enough on this issue to avoid debates and verbal sparring with those who stand by the old practice, for the campaign aims chiefly at educating and persuading those who allow themselves to be reached. Eventually the United States will join the other twenty-nine nations that have passed laws against corporal punishment, and when it does, this will become an added component to the persuasive mechanisms currently in place to guard the safety of children and the healthy survival of our society. For now we can view this as the most compelling and most satisfying of all endeavors.

## Accuracy in Historical Documentation

As the human race marches collectively towards an era of greater understanding and less conflict we come to realize more and more the essential role historians play in helping us transcend our current state and achieving loftier goals. That is why the issue of intellectual honesty takes on even more importance with historians for it is they who we depend on for an understanding of exactly what took place in the past. If these accounts are not accurate or if there are omissions of any sort, the analysis or conclusion of the reader may not be as accurate as it could be.

Omitting certain factors from the story is far less harmful than misrepresentations, but it still leaves room for improvement in the area of story-telling. In addition to the effort readers must make in understanding exactly what the writer is trying to say, it may be helpful to take a peek into the background of the writer if only for some additional information as to what shapes his or her thought pattern. This I believe, allow the reader to better grasp where the writer is coming from. With this an interpretation of the text may be more accurate.

In her book <u>Dangerous Games  The Uses and Abuses of History,</u> Margaret Mac Milan does a great deal towards accomplishing the goal of intellectual honesty. Her efforts to get us to analyze some of the reports of the past is extremely helpful, and as she introduce us to terms like Amateur Historian and Professional Historian, and the difference between the two, our care and analytical skills are enhanced. She tells us that: "History responds to a variety of needs, from greater understanding of ourselves and our world to answers about what to do."[1] Mac Milan goes on to say: "History has shaped humans' values, their fears, their aspirations, their loves, and their hatreds. When we start to realize that, we begin to understand something of the power of the past."[2] This brilliant assessment of history gives it added value as an important psychotherapeutic instrument. In all investigations, whether they are historic criminal or therapeutic, the question is always, what happened? This is because an accurate account of what happened empowers the reader, the investigator, or the therapist to go beyond the event and develop some clearer understanding as to how and why the events took place thus

---

[1] MacMillan, Margaret. <u>Dangerous Games, The Uses and Abuses of History</u> New York p 31.
[2] MacMillan, Margaret p 10

improving the chances of either preventing them or building on what was accomplished.

MacMillan conveys a sense of concern as she warns us against the dangers of ideologies in the form of Fascism, Communism, religious fundamentalism, and the unreasoning forces of ethnic nationalism as forces that challenge the assumptions of liberal internationalism.

In the past, and perhaps even in the present, many students saw history as a tedious endeavor, as they struggle to memorize names and dates, and to attach these to the events that are the subject matter of the course. MacMillan's approach has the ability to make history far more exciting than it has been known to be and bring more students into the study of history. We now look to the genesis of the event as well as its pathos, and we comment on the warning signs that could have helped to avert some to the atrocities of the past. Today, there are scores of documentaries and books depicting the life and times of some of history's most notorious criminals. The reasons are almost obvious and they are very much in line with some of MacMillan's insinuation; tell the truth of the events and don't be afraid to explore some of the facts leading up to them. Drawing this psychological inference from the text only highlights the importance of honesty in the actual recording of history. When it comes to recording history without the benefits of provable evidence, historians face an even greater challenge, for gaps in memory are commonplace with humans. She admonishes us that: "Memory…is tricky business…We mistakenly think that memories are like carvings in stone; once done, they do not change. Nothing could be further from the truth. Memory is not only selective; it is malleable."[3] The quote highlights the difficulty that is entailed in our reliance on memory in all forms of investigations including therapeutic. But neither can it be dismissed, as she reminds us on page sixty one in her book: "The absence of evidence to support a claim does not mean it did not take place."[4] This further reminds us of the enormity of the task that lie before investigators and others whose job it is to collect data, particularly on subject matters about which very little is documented. The recent debate over slave narratives is a good example of this. In the Donna J. Spindel article entitled: Assessing Memory, Twentieth Century Slave Narratives Reconsidered, the validity of the twentieth century slave narrative came into question as so many writers relied on them for historic accuracy. It stroke me that the article only mentioned the participants in the debate by their last name, not that this is of any great importance but any attempt to research the issue using these characters as reference would be made more difficult. That said, the principal character in the debate is one that goes by the name of Escott who apparently had come to rely heavily on these nar-

---

[3] MacMillan, Margaret p 33
[4] Mac Milan, Margaret p 61

ratives for his research. The issue of psychology and memory reliability in the aged was discussed extensively, with some arguing strongly that memory is not adversely affected by age, with both sides quoting a variety of scientific studies to drive home their point. The challenging point was the fact that Escott's study centered around the day-to-day existence of the slaves. Almost everyone agreed that the human mind can recall events at any age, particularly when they're connected to significant dates or periods in their lives. That memory can be relied on to some extent, but to rely on the slave's account of day to day affairs when they were only four five and six years old did appear unrealistic. Something similar applies in the field of psychotherapy; the patient or client is better at remembering the trauma and other poignant issues in their lives often with dates and times of day associated with them, but to recall daily events is always more challenging for anyone old or young. All of this serves to remind us that: "History must be written to remind readers that human affairs are complicated," [5] I would venture to argue that her efforts to simplify an otherwise complex task is met with great success reminding us of the fact that story telling is one of the oldest of human activities, and that getting the story right will elude us from time to time but the effort should not be abated, because in the words of the

---

[5] Mac Milan, Margaret p 81

great Spanish philosopher George Santayana: "Those who fail to remember the past are condemned to repeat it."[6]

Joyce Appleby, Lynn Hunt and Margaret Jacob have taken on this issue in a somewhat different way than Mac Milan and in some ways with even greater intensity. The fact that all the writers connected to this project surrounding the quest for historic truth are women may be purely coincidental, but it has great significance for me, a radical feminist who believes in the power of women, and their eventual role in making this a better world. The fact that there is so little writing dedicated to this subject makes their role even more important.

Over the years we've had glances of the healing powers of truth. It is demonstrated when all affected parties agree to exercise restraint and deal with even the most painful issues with some modicum of maturity. The new South Africa serves as a glaring and vivid example. Despite its multiple drawbacks it is widely believed that the Truth and Reconciliation Commission has played a significant role in the healing of that nation, and that it has cleared the path for them to move forward into a more harmonious and productive future. South Africa is still a long way from those lofty objectives, but there is no question in the mind of many that the committee averted a virtual blood bath, as the oppressed majority had to be held

---

[6] Mac Milan, Margaret p 93

back from taking reprisals against a minority that had ravaged their lives. The argument that truth and honesty are
necessary components for a society to come together appears to hold true but only to a limit. If justice, fairness and
a redistribution of ill-gotten gains are a part of the process
there is still a chance that the entire process may yet be met
with failure.

In their book, Telling the Truth About History, Joyce
Appleby, Lynn Hunt & Margaret Jacob introduce us to history through the prism of science. The first chapter of the
book is titled: The Heroic Model of Science, and in it they
walk us through the history of science from Copernicus
(1473-1543) to the Industrial Revolution with an abundant-
ly clear description of the mindset that accompanied each
stage of this development. Their explanations are complex
and intellectually challenging but within it we arrive at
some truths regarding our present reality and how it came
to be. In addition to Copernicus two other scientists played
a significant role in breaking the grip the church had on the
European society of the time. These were Giordano Bruno
(1548-1600) and Galileo Galilei (1564-1642). Copernicus
is credited with the heliocentric model for celestial bodies
but fear of reprisals from the church prevented him from
publishing his findings until he was near the end of his life.
Bruno in turn was defiant, not only did he publish findings
similar to that of Copernicus but he openly challenged the
church, refusing to recant and was burned at the stakes.

When Galileo published similar findings, he was denounced, imprisoned and even after recanting forced to spend his remaining years under house arrest. But the Genie was already out of the bottle; scientist and thinkers in Europe and elsewhere had learned of the heliocentric model and were challenging the church's authority on this subject. Many would argue that this sequence of events though spread out over more than a century, marked the beginning of the end for the dark ages. But the enlightenment age did not begin immediately after; strangely enough it was further research on the part of scientists in the protestant world that ushered in the enlightenment. It required thinkers and scientists the likes of Francis Bacon (1561-1626), Rene Descartes (1596-1650), Isaac Newton (1643-1727), Gottfried Leibniz (1646-1716), Emily Du Chatelet (1706-1749), Francois Marie Voltaire (1694-1778), Jean Jacque Rousseau (1712-1778), Denis Diderot (1713-1784), Mary Wollstonecraft (1759-1797), and Immanuel Kant (1724-1804) among others, to really usher in the new era, an era of science and reason. This new era would be marked by experiment, observation, mathematics and new forms of social communication. Established churches and religious dogmas were attacked: "as either deluded or upholders of backward looking tyrannies, ignorance, prejudice, and superstition."[7] This enlightenment was spread over Western

---

[7] Appleby, et al. p 33

Europe and some parts of the thirteen colonies that were later to make up the United States of America. Appleby, Hunt and Jacob report that one of the founding fathers was also caught up in the frenzy of the enlightenment:" Late in the century Thomas Jefferson expressed faith in the link between science and progress by ordering a composite portrait of the life size bust of Bacon, Locke and Newton."[8] They also paint us a picture of elegant homes of entrepreneurs, merchants and aristocrats of that same period, adorned with miniature planetary systems with movable globes circling the sun in elliptical orbits, made by skilled workers in copper and wood. I have paraphrased here, but the contrast of this image with slaves of the period being indoctrinated with the most repressive brand of Christianity is striking.

At the heart of the enlightenment was Newtonian science, and it was also a key component of the Industrial Revolution, but at the height of the celebrations, the authors inform us that: "the same people who taught of themselves as enlightened, as teachers and appliers of Newtonian mechanics were often the profit seeking promoters of steam engines, canal companies, or factory style manufacturing."[9] The leaders of the enlightenment saw science as a means to improving the lives of humans but before long it was limited to serving the interest of greedy industrialists.

---

[8] Appleby, et al. p 25
[9] Appleby, et al. p 23

In an effort to arrive at the truth about history, science appears to play a unique role. It helps us to understand how we got to this stage in our development. Twisting the truth in this endeavor would defeat the purpose, so in some ironic way we are nudged into honesty. The need to know and understand forces us to tell the story of human development as it really occurred.

A commitment to truth, in the telling of history can carry with it enormous inspirational capabilities. To think that in less than three centuries we went from the dark ages to an enlightenment period is impressive, especially given the fact that this period was followed shortly thereafter by an explosion in technology. Some of this development was detrimental no doubt, but in all, great lessons have been learned. We now discuss facts rather than beliefs, and the wholesale slaughters of the recent past are no longer commonplace. We may teeter on the brink of total annihilation from time to time, but the painful lessons of the past are now burned into the hard drive that makes up our collective desire for self-preservation.

Truth in history will remind us of our common ancestry as a specie, and though still resisted in many quarters, this factor is already playing a significant role in the healing process.

# Concepts of the Child

In this chapter I will discuss some of the concepts and theo-ries surrounding the issue of child development, particularly those concepts that focus on the role of experience in learning, in childhood. The theorists that are profiled in this essay are: John Dewey, Maria Montessori, Lev Vygotsky, Jean Piaget, and Erik Erikson. The views of these noted theorists will be com-pared and contrasted with that of one who preceded them all by more than a century, Jean Jacques Rousseau (1712-1782). I will attempt to explore whether any of these theorists derived any of their ideas from Rousseau or if they departed completely from Rousseau's thoughts.

Rousseau was chosen for a number of reasons, but chief among them is his unwavering commitment to the safety and security of children; at least as manifested through his writings. The controversies, and contradictions surrounding Rousseau's life also makes him a compelling figure for study and analysis for many scholars wishing to develop some understanding of or learn from the life of this enigmatic historic figure. Perhaps the most noted contradictions in Rousseau's life is his abandonment of his five children; none of multiple birth; to a foundling insti-tution never to see them again. Scholars must make extraordi-nary to understand or explain away these and other controver-sial aspects of Rousseau's life.

Rousseau is considered by many to be one of the first suc-cessful novelists, having rendered his opinions on children through two famous novels: *Emile* and *The New Heloise*. Rous-seau presents the ideas for his character Emile through a series of five books which have come to represent five of the stages of his character's life, and although, like Rousseau, the other thinkers and theorists dealt with in this report, all subscribe to the concept of stages in a child's development, this report will focus on the complexities involved in the adult child relationship described by Rousseau.

At a time when the concept of the child was not yet defined, Rousseau endowed the child, and particularly the infant, with almost magical powers in their ability to command the attention of those around them, and the enormous care that had to be invested in securing its safety. We find in Rousseau (1979):

> At birth the child cries; his earliest infancy is spent in crying. Sometimes he is tossed, he is petted, to appease him; sometimes he is threatened, beaten, to make him keep quiet. We either do as he pleases or else we exact from him what pleases us; we either submit to his whims, or make him submit to ours. There is no middle course, he must either give or receive orders. Thus his first ideas are of absolute rule, and of slavery. Before he knows how to speak he commands; before he is able to act, he obeys; and sometimes he is punished before he knows what his faults are, or rather; before he is capable of committing them. Thus do we pour into his young heart the passions that are later imputed to nature; and after having taken pains to make him wicked, we complain of finding him wicked (p.21).

Profound in its scope this analysis gives us as clear a picture of any other of the  complexities embodied in the infant child and the struggles of adults to relate adequately to this creature they themselves grew out of a few years earlier. This highly analytical and deeply psychological statement was made more than a century before the birth of the discipline we have come to know as psychology.

The dilemma that lies in reducing the powers the child holds, contrasted with the willingness or lack thereof on the part of adults to set this child free and allow it to grow unencumbered is one that will be dealt with in this book. In short, more liberty and less power, since the child neither requests nor has any need for the powers we attribute to it and it certainly is not happy when the other side of that power  is applied to him or her in the form of punishment or other corrective measures.

It is this dilemma that will be explored here as we assess the approach of other thinkers and theorists to this most complex of subjects.

With some degree of accuracy it could be said that this unresolved dilemma lies at the heart of much of the mistreatment meted out to children for all of recorded history, since in all that time as in the present, the specie struggled with devising efficient methods for raising children. That said, it can also be argued that Rousseau was one of the first to advocate for the safety and security of children, doing so without preceding theories or models that we know of. Thus the striking of a balance between the freedom which the child yearns, and those magical powers attributed to it that it never asked for, will be explored in

this book along with the opinions of others theorists and thinkers.

Mooney (2000) tells us that Dewey was born in Burlington
Vermont on October 20th, 1859 into a farming family. He studied philosophy at the University of Vermont from where he
graduated in 1879 with a degree in philosophy. Dewey went on
to do graduate work at the John Hopkins University where he
obtained a PhD in philosophy in 1884. After graduating, he accepted a teaching position at the University of Michigan.   In
1894 he was offered a position at the University of Chicago that
allowed him the opportunity to combine his teaching of philosophy, with two other disciplines: Psychology and Educational
Theory. Mooney (2000) tells us that within 2 years he had established the famous laboratory school that attracted attention
around the world. Dewey's Laboratory School established the
University of Chicago as the center of thought on progressive
education, the movement toward more democratic and child-
centered education. Mooney (2000), tells us that Dewey's position at the head of  the lab school was relatively short-lived but
created, in a few years, a wealth of educational research and
theory that continues do drive many of our best practices today
(p.2).

In Dewey (1916) we find a rather sober reference to youth
and our responsibility towards them when he argues that in directing the activities of the young, society determines its own
future. The nature of the child will largely turn upon the direction children's activities were given at an earlier period. Dewey
describes this cumulative of activities towards becoming a better person, as growth. (p.49) Dewey focuses on the powers chil-

dren possess for enlisting the cooperative attention of others, which he claims is another way of saying that others are marvelously attentive to the needs of children. That they are egotistical and self-centered before adolescence is not lost on Dewey, but it is his conviction that even in their egotistical self-centeredness there are moments when they are able to capture everyone's heart. Stable adults recognize that this power the child possess for garnering their attention is only temporary, and even their egotistical self-centered behavior becomes more tolerable because again it is only temporary. The travesty Dewy argues, are those adults too absorbed in their own affairs to take any real interest in children's affairs (p.52).

Mooney (2000) presents John Dewey's *Pedagogue Creed,* published in 1897. In its first and second articles Dewey makes reference to the power of children. He says "True education comes through the stimulation of the child's powers …The child's own instincts and powers furnish the material and give the starting point for all education" (p.4). Here Dewey speaks, not so much of the powers of the infant but of with the potential powers of the child in the learning process.

In what might be one of John Dewey's most significant statements we have in Dewey (1916), "From a social standpoint, dependence denotes a power rather than a weakness" (p. 52), for it involves interdependence, and a child's gift for social interaction, coupled with its dependency all tend to facilitate social responsiveness and social interaction. Rather than being in awe with a child and its immaturity, surreptitiously granting the child all of that unrequested power, Dewey (1916) argues that respect for immaturity can actually work as a perfect antidote for all that power we give to the child and the resentment that naturally accompanies it, for it is in the resentment that the attitude towards the child changes thus placing them in danger. Evoking the words of Emerson, Dewey (1916) implores us to respect the child, its space its right to solitude, for in the end respect for the child invariably translates to respect for self (p.62). But returning to the subject of freedom Dewey (1916) reminds us that the important thing to bare in mind is that it involves a mental attitude rather than an external constraint of movement, but also that this quality or state of mind cannot be achieved without a freedom of movement that allows one to explore, to experiment, and to apply all that has been learned. Applied to the child, this concept may allow us to envision a healthier society, one with less cases of depression, or aggression.

Mooney (2000) then introduces us to Maria Montessori, the Italian physician, and education reformer. Although she argued for educational structure, Montessori shared Rousseau's views that freedom and play constitute essential components in a child's development, and that it is in these unstructured activities that much of their learning takes place. That it is in this natural un-encumbered environment that the child gathers most of their valuable experiences. Like Dewey, Montessori attempted to bring about changes in the system of education, not only in her own Italy but also to anyone around the world willing to adopt her method.

Montessori subscribed to a more structured learning environment, one in which children begin formal learning at a very early age. In that she differs from Rousseau, but in ascribing more freedom and less powers to the child there was hardly any difference between them. In Kramer (1976) Montessori argue that freedom within carefully placed limits, and not authoritarian discipline, is the principle of education (p.7), and that is significant because the charges leveled at Rousseau by his critics is that he is willing to let children do as they please without any adult oversight or guidance. That overly simplistic approach to Rousseau on the part of his critics is effectively countered by Montessori when she suggests that this freedom ought to have carefully placed limits.

In Montessori (1912) we find a definition of freedom not as an external sign of liberty but as a means of education, and an overwhelming endorsement of Rousseau's views as it relates to the importance of adults respecting the child's freedom. Montessori describes the children in her school as the promise of things to come, and as the future of the specie: "They are the earnest of a humanity grown in the culture of beauty---the infancy of an all-conquering humanity, since they are intelligent and patient observers of their environment, and possess in the form of intellectual liberty the power of spontaneous reasoning" (p.84, 308).

Although the focus of this book is less power and more freedom, it is important to note that this does not preclude the natural powers the child possesses, not the ones given artificially to the child through misguided adults, powers they often remove at will, rendering the child in a lower position than powerless, it renders the child a victim. It is this natural power that is worth protecting. One such form of power, in Montessori's opinion, is the joy the child experiences when exposed to new knowledge.

It includes the power to learn from the environment by means of the senses. In Montessori's opinion these are important forms of power (p.301).

In a direct reference to Rousseau and the similarities between them particularly on the subject of freedom and liberty for the child:

> The school must allow freedom for the development of the activity of the child, if scientific education is to come into being...No one would dare to assert that such a principle already exists in teaching or in the school. It is quite true that certain pedagogues like Rousseau set out fantastic principles and vague aspirations of liberty for the child, but the true conception of liberty is, in fact, unknown to the pedagogues (p.7).

The similarities between Montessori and Rousseau on the question of less power and more freedom is clearly established in their writings and perhaps in the writings of most thoughtful thinkers who have argued for educational reform.

The Swiss theorist Jean Piaget rarely addressed the issue of freedom and power as it relates to the child but we do find in Mooney (2000) references to the similarities that exists between Piaget and Rousseau on the subject of more freedom for the child to play and learn as much as possible through that activity as she argues that Piaget stressed the importance of play as an important avenue for learning. Mooney (2002) also added, "It is largely the influence of Piaget, building on Montessori's work, that encourages uninterrupted periods of play in early childhood classrooms. When children are interested and much involved in a subject, they need teachers who respect this absorption with their work" (p. 62, 73).

In an interview with Jean-Claude Bringuier, author of the noted *Conversations with Jean Piaget,* Piaget argued that in the history of science and the formation of man's mind, determinism has played too much of a role, that there has been too few crossroads and too little by way of freedom. (p.102)  But in Muller (2008) we find a statement from Rousseau that appears to run contrary to the concept of freedom expressed earlier by Piaget, "Social transmission failed to explain why an individual may criticize collective beliefs in the name of human rights and truth, thereby contrasting the universal to the collective, i.e., truth to opinion " (p 12).

There are further contradiction emanating from Piaget in Muller (2008), when he tells us that according to Piaget the child first creates pretend play autonomously, through individual rather than social processes and through interaction with the environment rather than with people. This contrasts with the Vygotsky modeled soviet school that considers play to be essential (p.86).

The extended period for play which Piaget recommends, is the equivalent of Rousseau's concept of more freedom and both Rousseau and Piaget see play as an important part of the learning process. Piaget found no need to deal with the concept of power, concerning the child, because all of his time was spent observing them carefully, starting with his very own. This sharp and acute observation of children, along with his habit of engaging them verbally gave Piaget a special understanding of how they think and behave, thus removing from the equation the element of awe or the habit of conferring unrealistic powers to the child that are neither useful or requested.

Lev Vygotsky's work with children was not unlike that of Piaget as he too spent a great deal of time observing them and recording his observations. It is these observations that culminated in the theory he was able to put together, his noted theories on the subject of child development. The initial similarity Vygotsky holds with Rousseau lies in his embrace of children's freedom for endless play convinced that in play much learning takes play. Vygotsky rarely uses the word freedom but his emphasis on play and its importance inevitably invokes freedom since all play requires a level of individual freedom. Proposing the principle that children learn as much or more from the environment and from each other as they do from books or the curriculum, Vygotsky propose that children should have the freedom to create their own learning by choosing from the curriculum and from various classroom activities, the ones that best suit their needs and abilities. No doubt this level of freedom poses tremendous problems for teachers primarily because of class size and the challenge of evaluating the child's intellectual growth. That level of freedom proposed by Vygotsky must be matched with measurable results since when all is said and done, a child in the school system is expected to learn how to read, perform basic math and arithmetic, and conduct some basic reasoning.

We are told in Mooney (2000), that Vygotsky studied and responded to the works Sigmund Freud, Jean Piaget and Maria Montessori during their lifetime, and that he was greatly influenced by them, and that after graduating from Moscow University Vygotsky became a high school teacher, where his interaction with children and his careful observation of their learning peaked Vygotsky interest in the psychological aspect of the learning process. This careful observation of his own students in the learning process, lead Vygotsky to develop his first theory which he referred to as: The Zone of Proximal Development. Vygotsky described the Zone of Proximal Development as the area or distance that exists between the most difficult task a child can perform without the assistance of an adult or more advanced student, and the most difficult task a child can perform with that assistance (Mooney 2000, p. 83, 89).

Although this report is centered on a comparative between Rousseau and these five theorists/thinkers, the parallel that existed between Piaget and Vygotsky demands a closer look, and perhaps some more work by way of comparison.

Mooney (2000), tells us that Piaget was of the opinion that the child's egocentrism prevents it from perceiving the points of view of others thus making play less effective and more of a lone activity among these children. Vygotsky on the other hand, embraced the value of play as a valuable learning tool particularly when performed in a social setting (pp, 90, 91).

In addition to play and its relationship with freedom, knowledge and information also play a significant role in the development of individual freedom either for a child or an adult.

In a review of the interaction between the social world and cognitive development Lloyd and Fernyhough (1999), argue that scholars have long been interested in the relations between social factors and cognitive development. Lloyd and Fernyhough (1999), tell us that in his early work, Piaget

[1923/1959] argued that children below the age of 7are unlikely to benefit from social interaction, given the egocentric nature of preoperational thought. That children are like scientists, working alone on the physical, logical, and mathematical material of their world in order to make sense of their reality (pp. 311,321). Lloyd and Fernyhough (1999), also tells us that Vygotsky on the other hand believed that development, a social process from birth onwards, is assisted by others (adults or peers) more competent in the skills and technologies available to the cultures, and that development is fostered by collaboration within the child's zone of proximal development. They insist that Vygotsky's theory is the clearest example of a contextual theory which says that individual development cannot be conceived outside of a social world, and that social world is simultaneously interpersonal, cultural and historical. In other words, from a Vygotsky perspective one cannot consider social interaction between peers and between adults and children without understanding the historically formed social context within which that interaction takes place. Children's cognitive development is thus not the product of simply biological maturation, nor of interaction between them and others in their environment (pp. 311, 329).

The other term Vygotsky introduces is Scaffolding describing it as the assistance a child receives in his efforts to accomplish a particular task. We learn that the inspiration for the name is drawn from the technique of painters and construction workers who create extra flooring in the air in order to access a certain area in the work field. Vygotsky's ideas were considered controversial, particularly since he developed important psychological theory without any previous or formal psychological training.

Both the Zone of Proximal Development and the concept of Scaffolding introduced by Vygotsky represent examples of greater freedom the child can now access in his or her intellectual growth process.

Mooney (2000) closes this section of Vygotsky by telling us that for some teachers the idea that children can help each other learn is very freeing. They think back on the numerous times they've interrupted excellent opportunities for group learning by calling children to circle time where they are forced to sit and listen. Observing Vygotsky recommendations teachers have come to see that children learn not only by doing but also by talking, working with a peer and persisting until the task at hand is accomplished. It is this freedom to do and to learn through other means that Vygotsky strongly recommends (p. 92).

Erik Erikson is the last and youngest of these theorists introduced in this report and compared to Rousseau around the subject of more freedom and less power. Mooney (2000) tells us that he was born in Frankfurt Germany in 1902, that he was an artist and teacher who later became interested in psychology. Mooney also explains that Erikson's meeting and interacting with Anna Freud; the daughter of the great Sigmund Freud; played a role in persuading Erikson to study at the Vienna Psycho-analytic Institute where he specialized in child psychoanalysis (p.37). In a statement that may best define the notion of more freedom and less power Mooney (2000) presents Erikson telling us that parents, teachers and caretakers should learn to accept the  child's swing between independence and dependence, and reassuring them that both are okay (47).

To the subject of freedom Erikson dedicates the third of his eight stages of development, pointing to the child of three to six years old, a period in which we encourage their fantasy, their curiosity and imagination. Like Rousseau, Erikson refers to this period as a time for play, not for formal education although in Rousseau's case this period is far more extensive.

The other group to which Erikson dedicates much of his attention on the subject to freedom, are the adolescents, particularly those within that group that may be confronting identity problems. It is at this stage between the ages of twelve and eighteen Erikson claims, that the child is confronted with a variety of social and moral issues. It is here that Erikson (1980) introduces us to the concept of a psychosocial moratorium. In this moratorium, the adolescent will use experimentation to grant themselves a prolongation of the interval between youth and adulthood with the purpose of finding a niche in which he or she may fit comfortably (175). Taking some time out, traveling to Europe, taking some time out to smell the roses or just taking some time out to get to know themselves and formulate their own ideas about the world, with ideas removed from that of their parents, peers or their particular culture group. In the final analysis this might be the strongest advocacy for freedom by any of the five theorists presented in this report.

There is a genuine sense of honesty that emanates from those committed to the development of children, and this palpable honesty has the ability to maintain the interest of scholars and researchers on the subject. It can be said, without any attempt at boldness, that the future of the specie is largely dependent on the proper development of those who constitute future leadership. The survival of the specie for the foreseeable future may not be in question, what may be questionable is the quality of life in this projected future, and this is very much dependent on the attention we pay to the development of children.

The five theorists presented here have done their part, and no doubt future theorists will continue to modify and improve on what those before them have worked so hard to put together.

# SEXUALITY

Given the complexities surrounding the subject of adolescent LGBT exiting the foster care system, it may be helpful to begin with an attempt at some clear definition of sexuality at least as it relates to this chapter. I will begin with a statement from Walters (2007) that refers to sexuality in the United States as *a vibrant, rapturous, and intoxicating experience.* That statement is powerful enough to stand on its own, but the author qualifies it by adding that there is some ambivalence about the notion of sexuality, which has the tendency to truncate its value, since the statement really references only to those who are accorded a position of normativity. It represents only the young, the beautiful, those who are considered medically intact, and those that are psychologically adjusted. Those that fall outside the norm of these simple definitions; those such as the aging, and the sexually different; run the risk of mockery or even repudiation. This is the case of the LGBT community whose idea of sexuality and attractiveness runs contrary to many of the practices that are held sacred in our society. The very idea of tolerance; a right some in the heterosexual community feels they are in the position to grant to others; is by its very nature insulting. It reflects an ignorance of the nature of the natural differences established in the animal kingdom for creatures to manifest themselves. The refusal to engage the subject and to study it in depth speaks directly to the fact that the larger society is willing only to tolerate certain sexual manifestations even when they consider it to be abominable. Tolerance does not equate understanding, neither is it considered growth intellectually or emotionally, for the prejudices though not demonstrable, remain as strong and as real as it is with those who dare to openly demonstrate those same prejudices.

The larger society has traditionally reserved for itself the rights to oppress those who fall outside the norm bringing untold suffering to these individuals or groups who do not fit within that so called norm, but this same group that holds control over everyone else is unable to perform the type of introspection needed for recognizing its own sense of denial as it relates to its own reality. This same group, almost in mass, subscribes to the notion that a sky daddy (god) controls all of their actions and grants them the rights to be prejudicial with those who do not subscribe to the mandates of their sky daddy. This childish notion of God embraced by nearly all humans everywhere has made an elevated conversation on the subject nearly impossible, and the massive ignorance of the masses remains almost unchanged even in the face of extraordinary advancement in the area of technology. Gay, Lesbian, Bisexual and Transgender youths are being thrown out of their homes because of the way nature constructed them, and the one group that could lessen this burden by pulling the masses out of their darkest ignorance, has failed to do so. When we witness science teachers and other scientists bragging about their religious affiliations it is nearly impossible to imagine that there will be an entity that will eventually break the stranglehold ignorance has on the masses. The saddest part in all of this is when members of the LGBT community are made to participate in their own oppression. The one group that has everything at stake in confronting the male concocted set of beliefs has not yet found the strength to do so, instead it has sought desperately to modify these beliefs so that they too may fit under its umbrella. This form of self-oppression is hard to explain and one has to wonder why isn't there  more conversation on that particular subject in the LGBT community.

# EMPOWERING THE POWERLESS

The concept of empowerment is a relatively new one in our lexicon as traditionally, people never felt they had the right to be empowered. This concept was introduced in a massive scale by the young men and women leading the sixties movement as they demanded power for the people. A people that until that point had been completely powerless, and in nearly every sense continues to be just as powerless as they were a half a century ago. The question then continues to be: How do we go about empowering the powerless? A few thousand years ago some shrewd operators took on the mantle of Kings and Queens, and they somehow convinced the masses of the time, of their intrinsic superiority. This hypnotic control over the masses by an insignificant few lasted for thousands of years until the French revolution and others of its kind initiated a process in which that power would be arrested from those who claimed it for themselves. The process was bloody and untidy but eventually the masses came out on top. Some years later, we had some semblance of what was supposed to be a socialist revolution, one that was really designed to restore power to the masses. However, personality worship had already replaced the worshipping of the unseen and the unknown, giving individuals the opportunity to pose as gods, exercising the powers and privileges previously preserved for gods. That reality has lasted through our times albeit in different versions. In the United States and other capitalist countries, the CEO is the new god earning up to four hundred times more than the average worker does. In the previously socialist countries a few elites with a strong man at the top, have

66

succeeded once again at reducing the rest of their population to serfs and slaves.

The revolt of any oppressed group grants the rest of the population an opportunity to crawl out from under their own oppression as someone else is taking their lives into their own hands by confronting power. What is real however, is that these revolutions bring with them some confusion and some lack of clarity that makes it possible for them to be co-opted and re-routed before their potential or intended objectives can be accomplished. The Black liberation movement of the sixties, the Women's Rights movement of the seventies and the LGBT movement of our era are three of the most striking examples of a force that could have altered forever the stranglehold irrational childish belief has on the entire population. There is a growing atheist movement and some feel this may actually be the long awaited catalyst, but this group lacks the force and the passion to bring about any meaningful change. In addition, this group has not had to overcome oppression and discrimination brought on by their own natural identity. This book makes the claim that only an open challenge to the childish notions that drives all belief systems can really empower the masses freeing oppressed groups from the tyranny of the majority.

## SEXUAL FLUIDITY

As one who lists "builder" among his many activities, I am compelled to explore the opportunities that lie in this area for resolving a problem that really did not have to be. The basic cost of building material has remained relatively flat for the past few decades, and land near cities and most metropolitan areas has hardly increased in cost. It does not take much creativity to understand the potential of such a combination. Granted, the quickest answer may be that this community; The LGBT community; is not given for rural or suburban lifestyle but rather that they strive in the cities. The response to that is that opportunities reclaiming and rehabilitating properties also abound in cities throughout the United States. Putting these factors together in the most creative and effective way can and will have a positive impact on the issue of homelessness among adolescents emerging from the foster care system, and particularly the Lesbian Gay, Bisexual and Transgender elements within that particular group. In addition to that, the technology in building has made it possible for the costs to be reduced even less. Simple open floor houses and apartments can be completed for a fraction of the cost of a few years ago since the tools and machinery available to complete the task are much more effective in our times.

Given the audacity of the scriptures, its authors and its interpreters to condemn a certain portion of the human population because of their sexual nature  or their sexual fluidity, it seems odd that this group; the Gay, Lesbian, Bisexual and Transgender individuals would lend so much support to writings that are so nebulous, contradictory and unfounded. Both academia and the scientific community are grounded in facts and demand evidence for all that is written or asserted, yet on Sundays, or Sabbaths, as the case may be, these same individuals trade in their intellect and their reasoning for a set of beliefs with absolutely no connections to reality. For the LGBT community to follow suit is concerning, since in doing so they are contributing to their own oppression. The suggestion here is not that this group lead the masses to free the people of the world from the tyranny of religion; although it wouldn't be a bad idea; what is suggested is that this group exercise their rights to openly challenge the nonsense imbedded in the so called scriptures freeing those young men and women who are attempting to understand their sexuality and/or sexual fluidity from one of the primary reasons for their confusion.

# BELIEF

This section will analyze the neurological phenomenon of belief as it affects human beings in every culture and in all walks of life. It particularly focuses on this phenomenon as it relates to the benefits it may have brought to the species as a whole, or for that matter the role it may have played in holding back the overall development of the species. It is intended to be a sober analysis, devoid of partisan criticism or biases of any kind, in short it is intended to be a pure quest for understanding the aspects of human behavior that may have been affected by the phenomenon of belief. The sheer terror felt by some at the thought of disconnecting from their respective belief system will be analyzed in depth, for the purpose of furthering our understanding of the endless nuances connected to human behavior.

# RELIGIOUS INDOCTRINATION

Before embarking on the subject that encompasses the form of indoctrination most of us are familiar with; that is religious indoctrination; it is important to attempt a definition of the term itself and the various ways in which it has been utilized in the past. There is no question that over the years we have had a variety of definitions for the term. Barrow et, al (2010) comments that much of it depends on the academic level of the person offering the definition, or their political or intellectual inclinations. In offering a generalized and perhaps more generic definition for the term, we can safely say that it is a process in which coercion, persuasion and often compulsion, are used to introduce an idea or belief system to an individual or group of individuals. In this definition, a key component to the process invariably, is the absence of critical examination or questioning on the part of the new adherents. Barrow et al (2010), comments that the term has obtained a strong pejorative tinge in the educational discourse particularly because of the absence of critical thinking and questioning the term is associated with. Barrow et al (2010) tell us that the term is often contrasted with the grand ideas of autonomy and open-mindedness that our society has come to expect from any form of positive instruction (p. 279).

Religious indoctrination on the other hand, involves a particular effort to have its adherents submit to a prescribe set of narrow and irrational beliefs that invariably involves a concept of god as an image or person to be adored, to be in awe of, or to be fearful of. The proven and tested method is to implant these dogmas in the minds of the individual long before he or she achieves the capacity to discern the process for themselves, thus preempting all possibilities for resistance.

In their own analysis of this subject, Barrow and Woods (2006) introduce us to the term "unshakable belief", related to the intentions of the indoctrinator's intent. Getting someone to believe in a proposition that is lacking in proof or evidence is at the heart of the process of indoctrination. Barrow and Woods (2006) remind us that the essence of indoctrination is not to be found in the degree of conviction but in the blind unshakable commitment. It possesses something that is beyond argument, and beyond reasoning, that is its position as being antithetical to education (p. 71). Barrow and Woods (2006) tell us that there are things in the world that are different from education and even incompatible with it in certain areas, but indoctrination is education inverted. It involves denial of the value of rationality, a real phenomenon that we must contend with for reasons that are too numerous to list (p. 71). To be honorably committed to a cause is one thing, but indoctrination is clearly another level of functioning, one that requires much more of our attention. The term unshakable belief reminds us of the extraordinary efforts the neurological system had to make to accept irrational thoughts.

## THE RADICAL PERSPECTIVE

One of the features the three most influential religions in the western world (Judaism, Christianity and Islam) possess in common is that they are intricately connected to an area of the globe in which men communicated regularly with the Gods, or so we are told. Taken from the King James Version of the Christian bible the following are cases in which it is purported that God spoke directly to men:

*Leviticus 20*: **(1)** And the Lord spoke unto Moses saying. (2) Again thou shall say to the children of Israel, whosoever he be of the children of Israel, or of the strangers that sojourn in Israel, that giveth any of his seed unto Molech, he shall surely be put to death.

**Luke 12:42** And the Lord said, who then is the faithful and wise manager, whom his master will set over his household to give them their portion of food at the proper time.

**Exodus 33: 1** And the Lord said unto Moses, leave this place you and the people.

What is interesting about this is that in all of the references these are male Gods communicating exclusively with male humans. That in itself poses a profound problem, a problem that if addressed adequately may render all claims of these and any other religions meaningless. The fact that we continue to tolerate them all for so long despite the built in misogyny, and prescription for the treatment of children in the belief system they purport is surprising. The price we pay for such tolerance is not only on the increase in terms of numbers but also in terms of severity, since our modern technology has greatly facilitated criminal acts. With the combination of those two factors, our modern society is now witnessing the most horrendous criminal acts carried out with the greatest of ease. Ideological conflicts spawned by religious beliefs and fueled by religious fervor have added to the mix, only this time using children to carry out their biddings.

Christopher Reuter (2004) illustrates this point in his book *My Life as a Weapon: The History of Suicide Bombings,* with the following anecdote from the Iran Iraq war. The anecdote explains; at least in the case of Iran; the origins of the doctrine that made it possible for children to march happily towards martyrdom. The word Karbala is invoked for the first time and it is explained as the focal point of the division between the two major factions in the Muslim religion, the Shi-its and the Sunnis (p. 22). The story goes, says Reuter (2004) that upon the death of the prophet in 632 A.D., there was a dispute over who should be his successor since the prophet himself had not chosen one. His nephew and son-in-law Ali demanded the caliphate for himself on the grounds that only a blood relative could succeed the prophet. His supporters referred to themselves as Shiat Ali's party; however Abu Bakr, a member of Mohammed's circle took power instead. It turns out, according to Reuter (2004), the customs and traditions of the prophet went by the name of Sunna, and this was the name chosen by Abu Bakr and his followers, they referred to themselves as Sunny, thus the rivalry between the Shiites and the Sunny was born (p.22). What elevated the rivalry to its most dangerous point was a case in which a small squad of Shiites headed up by the prophet's grandson and third imam by the name of Hussein was trapped with some of his loyal followers in a town called Karbala, located near the Euphrates River. They had responded to the pleas of the rebelling city of Kufa whose inhabitants had supported his efforts to succeed the prophet. They faced a powerful and hostile caliph named Yazid but nobody from Kufa came to the aid of Hussein, so facing impending doom Hussein released his companions from their oath of fidelity, begging them to flee and save their own lives. Several of these supporters heeded Hussein's plea but seventy two remained with him and were all slaughtered with their leader. This self-sacrifice became the clarion call for all Shi'ites and the focal point of its religious indoctrination especially as it relates to children (p. 37).

We learn through Reuter (2004) that the story of Karbala held great sway for Shi'ites and was always a part of their sensibility and consciousness, passed down for centuries and retold in succeeding generations; reaching its peak when the neighboring dictator Saddam Hussein invaded Iran a year after the people of Iran rose up and threw out their Shah, Mohammed Rizah Pahlavi (p. 39). Reuter

(2004) tells us that the country's army was in disarray and unprepared for s a golden opportunity to enshrine his regime onto the pantheon of myth, describing it as a piece of good fortune and a gift from heaven, and that Khomeini used this to his utmost advantage. The Iranian people were cast in the role of proverbial seventy-two loyal followers, fully prepared to die, and this included its children (p. 42). According to Reuter (2004), at the time of the invasion and war declared on the nation by Saddam Hussein, Iran's army was still weak from the purges carried out against officers loyal to the Shah, and famous revolutionary guard was not yet formed. Only one item was in plentiful supply, people, and they were persuaded by Khomeini's regime that the best thing they could do was to die fighting their mortal enemy, the Sunnis. In order to find stocks of human cannon-fodder for the waves of attack, recruiters traveled through the schools. The story of Karbala was repeated in the form of an epic fairytale adventure, a grandiose stage on which they themselves were summoned to appear as heroes, as martyrs (p 44). Reuter (2004) gives us the description of one recruiter, who overwhelmed by the experience, fled to Germany where he later told the story. He reported that on some days entire classes were taken directly to the barracks by the revolutionary guards with families being informed that their sons had volunteered to go to war. If any of the children refused they were vilified and intimidated (p. 45). Every evening new child recruits would be standing in the barrack's yard distraught, intimi-dated with no real idea of what lay ahead. For ten hours each day the boys were taught to handle grenades and ma-chine guns, some did not even survive the first few days as they would often throw the grenade too late or in the wrong direction blowing themselves up. We drove dogs across the parade ground and shot them (p. 45). The chil-dren had to then catch the animals and slit their throats. Anyone who refused was given a ruck-sack full of stones and had to run with it on his back until he collapsed.

After a week, all the children were ready to kill the dogs. There were no family photos, no toys, no teddy bears, and no mementos ---nothing of their own, only a copy of the Qur'an on the narrow bedside table, and slo-gans of Khomeini decorated the huge dormitories. After their two-week training, the children had to function like machines, without fear, hope or feeling. We were instruct-ed by our superiors not to play with them else they would become children again; children who laughed and cried, and such children do not go to war. They hung a little "key to Paradise" around the children's neck and with this, sent them on to the firing line (p. 46). Reuter (2004) reports that between 1981 and 1989 when the stalemate between the two warring factions was declared, upwards of ten thou-sand children were sent to the line of fire and across mine-fields. They were sent, in order that their bodies would ex-plode all the mines clearing the field for the soldiers following them. The reasoning at the time was that donkeys were too stubborn to do the work these children were doing. According to Reuter (2004) one of the survivors later put on record: "we fought by throwing ourselves in front of the tanks, by leaping on the mines, by taking on the enemy with a stick or a rifle. We tried and tried but we did not become martyrs" (p. 47). Reuter (2004) ends this horrific narrative with the following newspaper report: "They crossed the minefields. Their eyes saw nothing; their ears heard nothing. A few moments later, you could see clouds of dust rising up. When the dust had settled again, you could see nothing more of them. Somewhere along the way in the landscape, there were scraps of burnt flesh and shards of bone lying all around" (p. 48). The paper then assured the reader that things had improved, since on this occasion it was reported that: "Before they step onto the minefields the children wrap themselves in blankets so their body parts don't fly in all directions after the mines are detonated. Then, they can be brought behind the front and carried to their grave in one piece" (p. 48). This anecdote is not irrefutable evidence of the impact of indoctrination on cognition but does highlight the power of indoctrination in getting the individual; and particularly the child; to act against his or her own best interest.

Reuter (2004) ends this narrative by telling us that everywhere---in every human society---children are comforted, cared for, protected and loved by their parents. Disabling this life affirming reflex and choosing instead to raise children as martyrs and to volunteer to kill themselves as well as others is certain to tear that society apart over time (p.15).

The attempt here was to highlight the indoctrination process, particularly on children and to raise the question of whether these self-sacrifices would have been possible without an effort to subvert the natural intellect of the child that leads to self-preservation and self-protection. The lack of intellectual stimulation appears to be a prerequisite in a child's willingness to submit to the form of indoctrination that leads to his or her abuse and as in this case, self-destruction.

In an article that appeared in the July 2009 issue of the *Evangelical Quarterly* entitled: The **Abrahamic** faiths? continuity and discontinuity in Christian and Islamic doctrine, Adam <u>Dodds</u> tells us that 'Abrahamic faiths' or 'religions of Abraham' is a popular designation for Judaism, Christianity, and Islam, emphasizing their common heritage. It denotes a 'family likeness' and a certain commonality in theology between Judaism, Christianity and Islam. This connotes a familial likeness between these three religions that trace their lineage back to the patriarch/prophet Abraham and the possible source of inspiration for this relatively new and useful designation (p. 230).

Writing for the July 2006 issue of the *Heythrop Journal*, Victoria Harrison also takes on the subject of the

Abrahamic religions by telling us that Judaism, Christianity and Islam provide their adherents with distinctive conceptual frameworks for understanding the world they inhabit; a worldview if you will, with great similarities between the three. This worldview however, has met its greatest challenge from modern science whose discoveries regarding the creation of the universe. On this subject they are at odds with each other holding diametrically opposed views (p. 348). Harrison (2006) goes on to emphasize that the success enjoyed by many branches of science in the twentieth century is no doubt largely responsible for the role it has come to play in modern intellectual life. Few would deny that one of the most remarkable features of the twentieth century was the unprecedented success of scientific method in providing explanations for many things that had previously seemed inexplicable. The results yielded by scientific method, which primarily involved the testing of theories by means of empirical experimentation, were often so impressive that many people came to regard science as the only reliable source of knowledge (p. 349). Harrison's comments remind us of the dilemma children, parents and educators are forced to contend with when confronting these new scientific revelations where the question is always whether to remain true to their faith or to open up to newly discovered knowledge. Harris (2005) suggests that religious moderates are themselves the bearers of a terrible dogma. They imagine that the path to peace will be paved once each of us has learned to respect the unjustified beliefs of others, and he attempts to demonstrate in his writings that the very idea of religious tolerance—born of the notion that every human being should be free to believe whatever he wants about God—is one of the principal forces driving us toward the abyss (p. 14). Harris (2005) then argues:

> We have been slow to recognize the degree to which religious faith perpetuates man's inhumanity to man. This is not surprising, since many of us still believe that faith is an essential component of human life. Two myths now keep faith beyond the fray of rational criticism, and they seem to foster religious extremism and religious moderation equally: (1) most of us believe that there are good things that people get from religious faith (e.g., strong communities, ethical behavior, spiritual experience) that cannot be had elsewhere; (2) many of us also believe that the terrible things that are sometimes done in the name of religion are the products not of *faith* per se but of our baser natures—forces like greed, hatred, and fear—for which religious beliefs are themselves the best (or even the only) remedy. Taken together, these myths seem to have granted us perfect immunity to outbreaks of reasonableness in our public discourse (p. 15).

Harris' sober analysis stands apart from that of others who could not resist the temptations of ridiculing the more irrational aspects of these belief systems. It does appear as if he understands that religion constituted a stage in human development that may have offered benefits to some of its adherents, and that at some point in its development the specie will realize that the process has more drawbacks than benefits. In that regard, Harris (2005) further commented that:

> Many religious moderates have taken the apparent high road of pluralism, asserting the equal validity of all faiths, but in doing so they neglect to notice the irredeemably sectarian truth claims of each. As long as a Christian believes that only his baptized brethren will be saved on the Day of Judgment, he cannot possibly "respect" the beliefs of others, for he knows that the flames of hell have been stoked by these very ideas and await their adherents even now. Muslims and Jews generally take the same arrogant view of their own enterprises and have spent millennia passionately reiterating the errors of other faiths. It should go without saying that these rival belief systems are all equally uncontaminated by evidence. Yet, intellectuals as diverse as H. G. Wells, Albert Einstein, Carl Jung, Max Planck, Freeman Dyson, and Stephen Jay Gould have declared the war between reason and faith to be long over. On

this view, there is no need to have all of our beliefs about the universe cohere. A person can be a God-fearing Christian on Sunday and a working scientist come Monday morning, without ever having to account for the partition that seems to have erected itself in his head while he slept. He can, as it were, have his reason and eat it too (p. 16).

Harris (2005) concludes his discussion on this subject by reminding us that the religious writings we hold sacred were really the work of sand-strewn men and women who thought the earth was flat and for whom a wheelbarrow would have been a breathtaking example of emerging technology. To rely on such a document as the basis for our worldview—however heroic the efforts of redactors—is to repudiate two thousand years of civilizing insights that the human mind has only just begun to inscribe upon itself through secular politics and scientific culture. The greatest problem confronting civilization Harris (2005 argues, is not merely religious extremism but rather the larger set of cultural and intellectual accommodations the larger thinking world has made to faith itself. This, Harris (2005) argues makes moderates largely responsible for the religious conflict in our world, because their beliefs provide the context in which scriptural literalism and religious violence can never be adequately opposed (p. 45). I close this section with Harris (2005), argument that, "A kernel of truth lurks at the heart of religion, because spiritual experience, ethical behavior, and strong communities are essential for human happiness. And yet our religious traditions are intellectually defunct and politically ruinous" (p. 222). Born in 1967, Sam Harris is part of a new generation of Americans with advanced intellect who has committed this intellect to combat the bias and other dangerous teachings emanating from the bible and other religious teaching. Harris has used his PhD in philosophy and neuroscience from UCLA to challenge many religious notions and to encourage people of his generation and others to think without fear of punishment or retaliation.

**Possible impact on the Child's mind**

In contemplating the Christian symbol of a gentle Jesus, meek and mild one has to wonder if the violent scenarios described in Reuters (2004) could be tolerated within Christianity. The stories of violence described in the first half of the Christian bible known as the Old Testament are a possible example of the similarity between the Abrahamic faiths and why this phenomenon may not be inconceivable and violence. Some examples of this are as found in the following biblical quotes:

*1 Samuel 6:19-20* And he smote of the men of Bethshemesh, because they had looked into the ark of Jehovah, he smote of the people seventy men, `and' fifty thousand men; and the people mourned, because Jehovah had smitten the people with a great slaughter.

***Isaiah 14: 21*** Make ready to slaughter his sons for the guilt of their fathers; Lest they rise and posses the earth, and fill the breadth of the world with tyrants.

***Hosea 9:11-16*** The glory of Israel will fly away like a bird, for your children will die at birth or perish in the womb or never even be conceived. Even if your children do survive to grow up, I will take them from you. It will be a terrible day when I turn away and leave you alone. I have watched Israel become as beautiful and pleasant as Tyre. But now Israel will bring out her children to be slaughtered."...I will ask for wombs that don't give birth and breasts that give no milk. The LORD says, "All their wickedness began at Gilgal; there I began to hate them. I will drive them from my land because of their evil actions. I will love them no more because all their leaders are rebels. The people of Israel are stricken. Their roots are dried up; they will bear no more fruit. And if they give birth, I will slaughter their beloved children.

***Ezekiel 9:5-7*** Then I heard the LORD say to the other men, "Follow him through the city and kill everyone whose forehead is not marked. Show no mercy; have no pity! Kill them all – old and young, girls and women and little children. But do not touch anyone with the mark. Begin your task right here at the Temple." So they began by killing the seventy leaders. "Defile the Temple!" the LORD commanded. "Fill its courtyards with the bodies of those you kill! Go!" So they went throughout the city and did as they were told."

*Leviticus 26:21-22* If even then you remain hostile toward me and refuse to obey, I will inflict you with seven more disasters for your sins. I will release wild animals that will kill your children and destroy your cattle, so your numbers will dwindle and your roads will be deserted. *Isaiah 13:15-18* Anyone who is captured will be run through with a sword. Their little children will be dashed to death right before their eyes. Their homes will be sacked and their wives raped by the attacking hordes. For I will stir up the Medes against Babylon, and no amount of silver or gold will buy them off. The attacking armies will shoot down the young people with arrows. They will have no mercy on helpless babies and will show no compassion for the children.

One is compelled to wonder about the effects strong and violent biblical statements have on the minds of children that are under the indoctrination of religion, particularly the Abrahamic faiths. Statements such as the following have to have had some impact on the child's mind unless they possess an extraordinary ability to completely ignore them when confronted with them in their study of the bible:

*Exodus 21: (15)* And he that smitten his father or his mother shall be surely put to death

87

***Leviticus 20* (2)** Again, thou shalt say to the children of Israel whosoever he be of the children of Israel, or of the strangers that sojourn in Israel, that giveth any of his seed onto Molech, he shall surely be put to death.

**Leviticus 20: (9)** For everyone that curseth his father or his mother shall be surely put to death.

**Leviticus 20: (13)** If a man lies with mankind, as he lieth with a woman, both of them have committed an abomination: they shall surely be put to death.

**Leviticus 21 (9)** The daughter of any priest, she profanes herself by playing the harlot, she profanes her father. She should be burned with fire.

Deuteronomy 17 (12) And the man that will do presumptuously, and will not hearken unto the priest that standeth there to administer before the Lord thy God, or unto the judge, even that man shall die.

***Deuteronomy 22 (20)*** But if this thing is true and the tokens of virginity be not found for the damsel: then they shall bring out the damsel to the door of her father's house and the men of the city shall stone her with stones that she die.

***Isaiah 13:15-18.*** Everyone that is found shall be thrust through and everyone that is jointed unto them shall fall by the sword. Their children also shall be dashed to pieces before their eyes, their houses shall be spoiled and their wives ravished. Their bows also shall dash the young men to pieces, and they shall have no pity on the fruits of the womb, their eyes shall not spare children.

Children brought up in the Christian tradition and instructed to read the bible are compelled to make sense of this aspect of their religion. The notion of an all-loving god comes into question for them and in many cases the entire foundation of their belief system crumbles.

The writings in these chapters and verses vary according to the version of the bible the person may be in possession of, thus, one is free to consult the versions of their choice or a few versions, for that matter, for the purpose of comparison. These writings contained in the bible have been condemned by some for their irrationality and dismissed by others as insignificant but rarely are they analyzed for the effects they have on the minds of the masses, particularly on the children's.

## The case of the FLDS and Joseph Smith (Dec 1805-June 1844)

It would be unfair to complete this book without a reference to one of the most polemical organizations in the United States and the plight of children within that organization. The organization in question is the FLDS, short for Fundamentalist Latter Day Saints, a branch of a religious organization first established in upstate New York by Joseph Smith.

Bushman (2005) tell us that Smith was born in Sharon Vermont in 1805 to parents Lucy and Joseph Smith, and that his family moved to Palmyra New York when Joseph was eleven. At the time the family moved there the region was a hotbed of religious enthusiasm, and like many people of that era both his parents and his maternal grandfather had visions or dreams that they believed communicated messages from God. Joseph shared that he had his <u>first vision</u> at fifteen, and that in it God told him his sins were forgiven. Around that time Joseph also reported being visited by an angel named <u>Moroni</u>, who revealed the location of a buried book of <u>golden plates</u> as well as other artifacts, including a <u>breastplate</u> and a set of <u>silver spectacles</u> with lenses composed of <u>seer stones</u>, which had been hidden in a hill near his home, that he attempted to remove the plates the next morning but was unsuccessful because the angel prevented him (p. 39).

Bushman (2005) reports that during the next four years, Smith made annual visits to Cumorah, only to return without the plates because he claimed that he had not brought with him the right person required by the angel. At the time Smith earned a living searching for precious metals; and in one occasion in 1826, he was accused of the crime of pretending to find lost treasure. It was during one of these treasure quests, he met <u>Emma Hale</u> who was later to become his wife. Smith then made claims that he was instructed by the angel that Emma was the right person and so on September 22, 1827  he succeeded in retrieving the plates  placing them in a locked chest. He said the angel commanded him not to show the plates to anyone else but to publish their translation, reputed to be the religious record of <u>indigenous Americans</u> (p. 51).

Bushman (2005) quotes Smith as saying that the <u>angel Moroni</u> took back the plates after Smith was finished using them.  The final translation named the <u>Book of Mormon</u>, was published in on March 26, 1830.  (p. 80)  Shortly after on April 6, 1830, Smith and his followers formally organized the <u>Church of Christ</u> with small branches developing in various counties of upstate New York.  As a result of the publication, Smith's fame began to grow, but so did the opposition to his work. Smith responded to this opposition by dispatching one of his followers by the name of Cowdery to <u>Missouri</u> in an effort to find a more suitable location for his church.  Smith spent the next few years in search of a more adequate place to establish his church building up a following in the process and by the summer of 1835 his following had grown from two to over fifteen thousand.  <u>Jackson County, Missouri</u>  had become the "center place" of what Smith considered <u>Zion</u> (p.162).

Bushman (2005) reports that jealousy over Smith's growing political power in the area prompted a mob of residents to physically attack Smith and Rigdon rendering them unconscious. The old residents resented the Mormon newcomers and the attacks continued, and even though

Smith and his followers attempted   to <u>patiently bear them</u> for a while, a fourth attack prompted a response on their part.  This action caused them to be expelled from the county (p. 109)

Bushman (2005),   also states that Smith hated violence but his experiences led him to believe that <u>his faith's</u> survival required greater militancy against <u>anti-Mormons</u> and Mormon traitors and before a cheering crowd of Saints, Smith declared that should there be non-Mormon attacks, Mormons would establish their "religion by the sword" and that he would be "a second <u>Mohammed</u>. His angry rhetoric possibly stirred up greater militancy among Mormons than he intended for it caused Mormons to go on the attack whenever they felt threatened by the larger community around them. As a result of this Joseph Smith became and was responsible for his followers behavior, and was under constant lawsuits and threat of incarceration. In all the strife, one of his followers <u>Brigham Young</u> emerged as one of Smith's strongest defenders and a promising leader (p. 346).

Brodie (1971) commented that under Young's direction about 14,000 Saints made their way to Illinois and searched for land to purchase.  Under rumors of secret polygamy and internal accusations of hypocrisy many of the followers began to consider Smith a fallen prophet, causing him to spend considerable time and energy trying to convince them that he still had their key to heaven (p. 245).

Bushman (2005) tells us that Smith's followers gathered on the banks of the Mississippi and Illinois welcomed them with open arms.    Smith purchased high-priced swampy land and urged his followers to build their homes there as he was busy promoting the image of the Saints as an oppressed minority, even going as far as petitioning the federal government for reparations (p. 381).

Bushman (2005) tells us that the group settled in the western corner of Illinois calling their new community Nauvoo,   which is Hebrew   for beautiful. The charter granted the city virtual autonomy, and that itself may have been the root of more of Smith's self-destruction as he became emboldened enough to put together a Legion of armed men of his own. The charter also authorized the Nauvoo Legion an autonomous militia and Smith appointed himself Lieutenant General controlling by far the largest body of armed men in Illinois (p. 222).

We further learned from Bushman (2005) that in April 1841, Smith secretly wed Louisa Beaman as a plural wife, and during the next two and a half years he may have married thirty additional women, ten of whom were already married to other men, and about a third of them teenagers, including two fourteen-year-old girls, all of this while vehemently denying any advocacy of polygamy. Smith told at least some of his potential wives that marriage to him would ensure their spiritual exaltation.  Although Smith's first wife Emma knew of some of these marriages, she almost certainly did not know the extent of her husband's polygamous activities. Smith kept the doctrine of plural marriage secret except for potential wives and a few of his closest male associates (p. 437).

In 1844 an exposé of Mormon polygamy was published and Smith permitted his followers to destroy the defectors press. This created even more animosity towards the Mormons and in their retaliation a riot ensues. The Illinois governor intervened by sending in a militia to arrest Smith and charge him with inciting a riot.

Bushman (2005) offers a more dramatic depiction of the events surrounding the last few hours or minutes of Smith's life telling us that an armed group with blackened faces stormed the jail and killed Hyrum instantly with a shot to the face, that Smith fought back with a pepper-box pistol that had been smuggled into the prison but was shot while jumping from a window, then shot and killed as he lay on the ground (p. 549).

In Jessop & Brown (2009) Flora Jessop one of the victims who escaped to tell her own story, is a strong example of how religious indoctrination severely hampers the intellectual development of children and facilitates their sexual abuse. After describing the ongoing social and political upheaval around the time of her birth in 1969, the fourth of seventeen children, Jessop then contrasted that with the isolation of living in the desert cut off from the rest of the world in a religion that had established its own rules and its own code of conduct. Chief among these rules she tells us, is that only the men in the religion had a direct line to god, and that they were to take many wives and father many children. For this they were to receive everything they needed on earth and the promise of glory everlasting. The wives experienced the privilege of doing their husband's bidding all of their lives on earth, and moving aside to make room for their more fertile--- and younger sister wives when they grew too old to have children. But that was ok since they were promised the privilege of serving their husbands in the afterlife, for eternity. Flora goes on to tell a horrifying story that begins with a post baptism scene:

>As I stood there in the cold, newly baptized and wholly miserable, I didn't think things could get much worse. But they did, and fast. For me and many other children in Pligville, baptism marked not only the end of our childhood but the end of innocence. Husbands and fathers may not have been as exalted as the prophet but we all knew that god spoke through them, at least that's what we were taught to believe...But a few days after my baptism something changed all that forever... I had already started cutting down the arms and legs of my sacred garment and that day I decided I wouldn't wear it at all...I wandered down to the barn to see my favorite pony. I expected to be alone so I was surprised to

see my father there…Even though he was my father I'd never felt comfortable around him…I had watched him beat my brothers without mercy…Hey Flora come on over here…He was never nice to me…Why was he being so nice to me now?….I was a tiny eight year old…He reached out for me and put his hands underneath my dress. I wanted to run home to my mother but I couldn't move…I couldn't imagine why he would ask me to do this. But he was my dad---the priest of our home. What he did was commended by god, so he must have a reason. Anyway, I knew what could happen if I didn't do what he ask. I couldn't even breathe. I was terrified that someone would walk in and see us but I wasn't even sure we were doing something wrong. Then he put his rough dirty hands on my vagina, unbuttoning his pants and yanking them down…My face felt hot and my mind was racing. I didn't know what was happening. I sat perfectly still numb with shock, fear, humiliation and confusion…I thought it would never end… Button up he said, get out of here Now…My dad's abuse became a regular part of my life…he made my life hell (p. 9).

Jessop & Brown (2009) commented that in June of 2009 after the bungled raid on FDLS compound and the Texas judge ordered the children to be returned to their conditions, Jessup spent a month traveling around Texas and visiting many of the facilities that housed the free children. She spoke with care-takers, Child Protective Service workers, of Texas Rangers, and many others. She was told by one foster family that twelve of the children, ages ranging from four to thirteen were placed in their care for three months. Ten of the twelve had been victims of sexual abuse, and three of the boys had such severe rectal damage that they had no bowel control. A thirteen year old girl had already given birth to a child, and one of the boys had already suffered from nineteen broken bones. The excuse given was that the mothers of these children had completed a two hour parenting class and had signed a paper stating that they now understood what abuse was. Jessop described CPS workers reporting to her, with tears in their eyes, a scene in which workers literally had to push some of the children across the room, while they were begging not to be returned to the religion. Many of the mothers who were hoping to follow their children in escaping their enslavement, now had their hopes dashed as a result of the government's deplorable actions (p. xi).

In the July 25, 2004 issue of the online magazine *Religious Tolerance.org* writer B.A. Robinson quoted Utah state Senator Ron Allen as saying:

> We have thousands of women pulled out of school at an early age, forced into marriages with older men, kept isolated from society, constantly impregnated, and often placed on public assistance with no

financial means of their own. They are forgotten citizens facing abuse and fear. On top of it all, the victims are constantly taught that God is just pleased as
punch about the whole deal. It has to stop (p. 1).

On the same subject and in that same issue of the magazine Salt Lake City writer John Llewellyn, a former member of a Fundamentalist Latter Day Saints restorationist
denomination offered his own analysis:

The key factor in controlling a polygamist religion
is in brainwashing the young women to inculcate
upon their impressionable minds that everything not
condoned by the prophet is evil, that they cannot go
to the celestial kingdom unless they live in a plural
marriage, and that the gates of heaven will be closed
to the disobedient (p.1).

In addition to the cases of sexual molestation many of
the boys suffered the horrible fate of being kicked out of
the only home they ever knew, as in the report from Jessop
& Brown (2009) in which Flora claimed she had an additional worry when she turned fourteen that was, being assigned a husband. They tell us that every FLDS girl understood that as soon as she turned twelve, she could be married off at the whim of the prophet. To decrease the competition and satisfy their twisted desire for multiple wives
the prophet's council of old men were in the habit of kick-
ing teenage boys off the compound, and that the number of
these lost boys are in steady increase (p.73).

The previous two comments out of Utah seem like a good note on which to end this analysis of what we may refer to as the Mormon phenomenon and the effects it may be having on the children within that religious structure. This one hundred and fifty year old phenomenon has been largely ignored by academia and the media perhaps because of its apparent religious nature, but the growth of the religion and its heavy-handed global proselytizing makes it a force to be reckoned with, analyzed and understood.

If children are to be saved from the abuse of Mormonism, and particularly the fundamentalist arm of the Mormon religion, part of the deprogramming or liberating process should include the reality behind the life and times of the prophet they are made to believe in. This applies to the Christian religion and any other religion for that matter. Demystifying religious icons is an important step in convincing children that there has never been in the history of the human race, a being with a greater intrinsic value than the others who compose the group. When they become persuaded of this they may well experience what it is to do good just because it feels good and not because of some religious icon or instructional book. There is also a good chance that they will be less prone to intimidation and as a consequence, less vulnerable to abuse. Weighing down a child's mind with fear and superstition is no way to achieve intellectual development, as intellectual development requires freedom to think and explore.

If the species is to advance intellect will have to play a greater role than it does today. Much has been said about the fancy gadgets children are exposed to today and their extraordinary abilities to master these gadgets in zero time, but some doubts remains as to whether this has had much effect on the intellectual growth of these children, and their sense of independence as individuals. Although there are hardly any signs of organized resistance on the horizon, it is hard to imagine the species holding steadfast to these discredited belief systems for much longer, but highlighting the damage they continue to cause on young minds appears to be perhaps the one inevitable way of confronting a structure that has been so effective in slowing human growth and bringing so much misery to so many over the ages.

As we embark on this quest to understand human behavior, particularly as it is affected by belief or belief systems. It is important to recognize that for reasons beyond our explanation, there is precious little data available on this subject. One gets the impression that the power to ostracize those who dare to openly criticize the phenomenon of belief remains an ever-present deterrent for scholars who by their own nature have resisted the power and control held by religions of all sway even in our era of modernity. The data available on belief and its effect on human behavior, particularly its effects on human brutality is scant, a factor that causes this research to be all the more challenging, for despite its importance and the enormous effect belief has had on the human psyche, as well as on human behavior, scholars everywhere have avoided this issue at all cost. This seemingly collective decision; at least at a subconscious level; has had the effect of leaving the masses in every culture and in every society, up to their own devices. They have been left to figure out the conundrum of belief all on their own. These masses that appear to reside in a permanent state of confusion about nearly everything in their lives, are left to make sense of something as complex as religion, dogma or belief. Since the brightest among them avoid the subject, they are left to figure out this subject on their own despite the confusing quandary in which nearly all happens to find themselves in, particularly as it relates to this subject. It has been said that to believe is to submit one's self to suggestion, something akin to being under the spell of a skillful mind operator or mind manipulator, and it is that very aspect of belief that I will be exploring in this book. It can therefore be said, that this book is another effort to understand the powerful spell under which the overwhelming majority of the species we have come to know as humans, has allowed itself to be held under a spell, perhaps dating back to the early period in which it began to describe itself as civilized. My position as a nonbeliever allows me to examine this subject thoroughly without any concerns for those who may be offended by the findings, or by the analysis that emanates from these findings.

It is nothing short of interesting that Harris *et al* (2009) would argue that the industrial world anticipated the demise of religion as we know it given the extraordinary promises of technology and a more advance way of thinking as it was expected. For reasons that are nearly impossible to explain, this turned out not to be the case. This prompt the researchers to delve into the phenomenon of belief and the mechanisms involved in the stranglehold it has succeeded in maintaining over nearly all of those who refer to themselves as humans. According to Harris *et al* (2009) there appears to be a continuous correlation between culture and religion although the authors fail to give us any definition for either of those terms. It behooves us then to pause and attempt to identify these terms before we advance in this discussion thus I shall refer to religion as the process through which human beings attempt to identify with the forces responsible for their existence, and for that same purpose I shall define culture as "learned behavior." As we proceed with these simple definitions we recognize that the guess work has been taken out of the subject. Harris *et al* (2009) suggestion that the human mind may be predisposed to harboring religious beliefs is indeed awakening but he posits the question as to why cultures like that of the Japanese, the French and the Swedes refuse to succumb to the childish notion of the God of Abraham

embraced by most of western Cultures. What I find interesting in all of this is that Harris *et al* (2009) refers to the
brain as an evolving organ seeking to achieve higher order
regardless of the intellectual limitations of its immediate
environment. While we engage in definitions it may be
useful to include faith, and the opinion we may hold of that
term. Again for the purpose of this book faith is defined as
blind belief, or a strong belief on something for which
there is absolutely no evidence.

There is an element of wonder regarding the survivabil-
ity of religion as a construct that provides guidance for
human behavior and interaction. This is even more so in
the industrial world where it had long been assumed that
with the acquisition of further knowledge and the spread of
technology, humans in general may finally achieve freedom from religion along with the mythology and limited
thinking it appears to have built into its fibers. Thus, the
predicted death of religion as we know it, turned out to be
rather premature, prompting further curiosity on the part of
some scholars to further delve into the study of this phenomenon and the powers it sways over masses everywhere.
It brings to mind Karl Marx's famous remark that religion
is the opiate of the masses as he equated it with the con-
suming powers of a powerful drug that people in general
could never have enough of. What we do know however is
that Marx never had the luxury scholars and scientists possess today to study the human mind in order to accurately

understand the reason for our dependency on a construct that fits into no rational model. The research begins with the acknowledgement that for all the importance we have given to religion in nearly all societies, we know precious little about the mental source for this phenomenon and the reason why humans feel the need to be attached to it in some form or another. Contrary to the predictions made at the turn of the century, the strength of dogma and religion appears to be gaining footage in some parts of the world. The advances in technology are now allowing us to pierce into the brain to observe reactions in individuals who are attached to religion, for detectable internal reactions to the many emotions that are provoked by the attachment to religion. The Magnetic Resonance Imaging or MRI, and the Electro Encephalogram or EEG are but two of the scientific instruments in use today to facilitate detection of brain reaction in people that are strongly attached to some form of religion. Some connections have been made by these scholars and scientist with the serotonergic system of individuals who are deeply involved with religion. Having identified Serotonin as one of the principal neurotransmitters responsible for feeling of well-being in the individual they've identified a series of drugs that in their opinion play a role in also driving the religious experiences sought by many individuals. Harris *et al* (2009) inform us that drugs such as LSD, Ecstasy and Mescaline, to name a few; have proven to be rather potent drivers of religious/spiritual experiences in some individuals. The rites, rituals and customs practiced within the enthralls of many of these religions makes the task of studying them and their effects even more daunting. Some neuroimaging study of belief as a general mode of cognition were conducted and studied but these studies are far from being conclusive. These scholars seek to understand at what point in our evolutionary process did we develop an attachment to religion and religious concepts, and whether there is some genetic explanation as to why some cultures appear to be more attached to religious concepts than others. One would not dispute the influence of religious doctrines that purport to be true, and their subsequent acceptance as true by great numbers of human beings, but that factor alone does not answer the question as to why this happens to be so.

Norman et al (2008) tells us that the human mind possesses a limited capacity for processing information, and it may be fair to say that this may just be the central point of why dogma and belief in the hands of skillful manipulators, have been able to maintain such grasp on humans everywhere. Norman et al (2008) also introduce us to the term *Poetic Faith* as a way of describing the trancelike state in which humans generally fall into the moment they adopt one of the plethora of faiths by which they are continuously bombarded. The authors compare it to the feeling one experience when transported by a literary work where we are influenced to suspend our disbelief, our incredulity and our sense of suspicion that something here may not be right, something here just does not add up and that I may in fact be in the state of being manipulated. In the opinion of Norman et al (2008) a prolonged adherence to these unfounded notions has the potential for producing in the individual a sense of delusion, and they describe delusion as an island of irrationality. The question to be asked is, at what point do we allow irrationality to govern the affairs of humans? The reason for this question lies in the fact that nearly everywhere today the individuals who postulate themselves as political leaders must pass a litmus test that includes an adherence to a particular dogma, and invariably it must be the most popular dogma at the time in that particular region of the world. In the United States we understand that litmus test all too well as it manifests itself in the pandering politicians are forced to subject themselves to in order to gain the votes of the multitude of individuals that describe themselves as religious.

In describing the general penchant for fiction that appears to run common in all humans Norman et al (2008) explains that we embrace only a portion of the information that is fed to us by way of fiction, that even though at first we appear to believe it all, as some degree of rationality imposes itself we begin to drop some of what is just too obviously ludicrous. Norman et al (2008) also introduce us to the opinion of Rene Descartes on this issue who argued that ideas are accepted in two stages, the first being an effort to comprehend them; which unfortunately demands a level of acceptance. This, fortunately, is followed immediately or sometime after by some form of examination to determine if it is true or false. But it is fair to say that the brain can do but so much, constantly bombarded by information that purports to be true the job of determining this for themselves can prove to be overwhelming for the individual human mind, and in failing to carry out that task accepts the default position that if it is written or if it is spoken especially by a supposedly authority figure, it must be true. It is perhaps the reason why Norman et al (2008) made the argument that human beings in general are very poor at ignoring, our curiosity leads us to pay attention to all that we see and hear, and our credulity leads us to accept much of it as truth. This tendency to believe everything we see and hear without thorough examination may be the principal cause for what we have come to regard as prejudice, the kind of prejudice that spawned inhumanity and unspeakable suffering to millions over the millenniums. There are those who would argue that the kind of suffering we witnessed in the past century, made easy of course by weapon technology and advanced techniques for murdering many at a time; could easily repeat itself if we continue to fail at conducting the necessary thorough examination of the issues we are presented with. The Jewish holocaust and the African holocaust of the middle passage may just be examples of the potentials we possess for cruelty at a massive level. Our advances in technology may in fact allow us to carry out those atrocities with greater ease. The cause for alarm on this issue is spurned by the fact that human intellectual growth  has not kept pace with technological advancement, instead what we are witnessing is a rise in overall prejudice and hubris, and if these two are inspired by ignorance; as we've been told; then the capacity for greater may have increased almost exponentially. Ignorance reign supreme among the masses, despite the widespread availability of advanced knowledge, and this is cause for alarm especially when these ignorant masses exercise their penchant for placing absolute power in the hands of those that are even more ignorant and more unstable than themselves.

From the standpoint of neurobiology Norman et al (2008) explains that belief comes easy and is natural with us, while disbelief on the contrary , must be actively constructed . Norman et al (2008) also reference Gerrig's extensive experiments on the subject where he concludes that some element of belief must occur when the individual subjects him or herself to a narrative; it is referred to by some as suspended disbelief or suspended judgment.   In some cases the situation is corrected when the individual decides to examine the case they're confronted with but too often than not this second step never takes place and the suspension of disbelief becomes permanent. Examples of this suspended disbelief is everywhere in our society, and it is the feeling of some that the very poor thinking that spawns the lack of examination is also responsible for the resurgence and strengthening of prejudice in areas where divergent racial and cultural groups must compete for the resources in their societies. Of course this is particularly so in societies whose economy is purely profit driven as the absence of a social or economic safety net has the potential to make matters worse for the individual and the group. The irony of the trance like state experienced by believers is not lost on researchers, and it explains in part the reason why religion continues to maintain the power it has over such a massive portion of the human family.

In an attempt to make sense of this paradox Hobson (1995) argues that it is a natural part of our survival mechanism that we take the time out to perform the first action as it relates to an idea, which is think and examine those ideas in detail. That only when we take the necessary action in regards to an idea that it really becomes our own. The common expression "tell me anything I'll believe it" seems to take on real life as we delve into the functioning of the human mind in this case, for now we know the poetic nature of the expression, that we do in fact give credence to everything we hear, particularly when it presented with authority. It is not until we embark on the difficult task of examining that idea or concept that we allow ourselves to

reject it wholly or in part. Despite Hobson (1995) proclamation that the brain's principal objective is to assist the
individual in identifying with the real world, and that it
does this to guarantee its survival in addition to enhancing
its reproductive capacity;  there are not that many humans
who really live up to this proclamation. The notion that
taking action or a plan to take action actually constitutes
testing of that reality may be misleading if the action in
question does not entail a thorough examination of the idea
presented. If the action taken is simply to go along with
what is presented, or as Norman et al (2008) describes it, to
fall into the trans like state the masses delight themselves
in falling into, then it is hard to see how said action actually tests reality. It is hard to see how an automatic embrace
of an idea or concept could constitute testing since we
equate testing with examination, dissecting, and putting
something to test, not embracing.

On a personal note, I have wasted a lifetime in a futile
attempt to organize the masses of black people, and people
of obvious African ancestry towards their own socio economic growth. What I failed to understand during this effort was the trans like state or hypnotic state in which the
slaves were to remain several generations after they were
set free. This inability the examine the belied system imposes on them by their former slave masters has doomed
them to failure, and there is none among them with the in-
testinal fortitude to state that fact.

For an example of how belief enhances prejudice one could cite the case of the Central Park Jogger that took place in the city of New York twenty four years ago. In this case a white female investment banker was beaten, raped and left for dead in the park, and a group of minors who happened to be wasting away their time in the park that night were identified as the culprits and charged officially with the crime. Those whose parents understood the law and argued that their son's *Miranda Rights* were violated, were able to get off free, but in five of the cases police interrogators in the city of New York were able to manipulate them into confessing to a crime they did not commit. They did so by depriving the kids of food and water for more than 24 hours, while telling them in separate interrogations, that he was fingered by the others as the culprit. The entire city was led to believe that these minors committed the heinous crime with many, including Donald Trump arguing for a return of the death penalty so that it may be applied to these minors. After serving nearly a decade for a crime they did not commit one of the minors was able to make contact with the real culprit of the crime, who confessed to him and then to the authorities. No apologies came from the press that condemned them in the eyes of the public or from the individuals who so loudly proclaimed their guilt. To add insult to injury the city has refused to honor the group's request for compensations due to false imprisonment. There is no doubt that the element

111

of race played a strong role in this case but so did belief. The entire white population of New York, and most of that of the other groups in the city was swept up in a trance-like state induced by authority figures who were able to present a convincing case against the young men. It did not matter that the DNA evidence collected at the scene did not match that of any of the accused. The use of DNA in crime cases was relatively new at the time but it was touted as completely reliable, both for conviction, and for exoneration. In this case however, DNA suffered suspended disbelief on the part of nearly everyone who followed the case, as blinded by hate and prejudice, the detectives, the prosecutors and the district attorney decided against finding a match for the DNA sample they had gathered. To obtain a conviction the authorities in New York relied solely on the confessions they were able to pry out of these minors without their parents or an attorney present. The rest of New York and the country bought the entire manipulation, hook, line and sinker. I remember at the time arguing that without a DNA match these people could not be that devilish to charge these kids with murder. It was a mob like atmosphere with Donald Trump, the mayor of New York Edward I Koch and the governor Mario Cuomo leading the pack. It was as Norman et al (2008) describes it, a willingness to suspend disbelief, only that in this case it was occurring at a massive scale in a very modern period.

For another point of view, I must again point to Norman et al (2008) and their reference to the philosopher Emmanuel Kant. Kant they claim, argued that there is a certain level of harmony between the usually conflicting ideas that occupies the human mind, and that the individual derives a certain element of pleasure from this unseemly relationship. The passive state of mind during which we receive information also adds to the credibility we lend to it, the not having to or planning to act is a determining factor, not unlike the example presented by Norman et al (2008) offering us the comparison between watching a movie at the theater and watching that same movie on a DVD. At the movies, one is part of a captive audience, virtually imprisoned by the circumstances at least for those few hours, and the sense of criticism is almost nonexistent during that period. That same movie watched on a DVD allows us the freedom to criticize, to stop and to examine aspects of the film that we would not have noted at the theater. The sense of empowerment we feel when watching a movie at home makes all the difference in the experience. The operative word here is empowerment, and expression in need of a great deal of examination, only because it is its absence, the absence of power, that plays such a pivotal role in the extent to which some humans will be subjected to suffering and injustice. Politics and Economics immediately springs to mind when we use the term empowerment but in this case I'm referring to the empowerment that is

113

developed in the individual as a result of being fed factual, evidence based and useful information. This is the type of information that can be processed by anyone, including children, but it is precisely the kind of information they and the rest of the population is used to receiving so little of.

Notwithstanding its extraordinary influence, belief still has its silent detractors among its adherents, and this too we seldom hear about. In *Troubled Faith*, Zygon (2007) makes reference to the noted christian devotee Teilhard de Chardin (1881-1955) who agonized over his expressed ambiguity as he questioned whether a Universal Christ is really a fact, whether the divinity we have all been sold on really has any basis. Zygon (2007) tells us that another devotee who came to question her faith before her death was Theresa of Calcutta. Zygon (2007) referenced Father Brian Kolodiejchuk, a leading advocate for Mother Theresa's canonization who is said to have reported on some of the disclosures made by Theresa of Calcutta. Father Brian spoke of her feelings of doubt, loneliness, and abandonment by the God she long adored.

St. Pierre and Persinger (2006) delivered a report of 19 major studies they conducted over a period of 15 years in which they found that sensed presence, a feeling of a Sentient being, can be experimentally produced within the laboratory. This experience, they claim, is enhanced, and is produced more frequently when the appropriate fields are

applied through the temporal lobes with a particular emphasis on applying these fields over the right hemisphere
of the brain of the experimenter. St. Pierre and Persinger
(2006) prefaced their findings by stating that if all experiences are generated by brain activity, then experiences of
God and spirits should also be produced by the appropriate
cerebral stimulation, and this precisely is what the researchers had set out to prove. They recognize that these
phenomena are manifested more frequently in people
prone to complex partial epileptic seizures involving the
temporal-limbic regions, or patients who have sustained
"mild" brain traumas. The authors demonstrated that the
sensed presence of a "Sentient Being" can be reliably
evoked by very specific temporal patterns of weak trans-
cerebral magnetic fields applied across the temporo-
parietal region of the two hemispheres of people already
with a high level of suggestibility who are also perceptible
to exotic beliefs. To further our understanding of their
experiments St. Pierre and Persinger (2006) explain that
the sense of self and the appreciation we experience for the
self of others are derived from the subtle but complex
structural and neuro-electrical differences between the left
and right hemispheres of the human brain. The experiment
is aimed at facilitating intra-cerebral intercalation through
the corpus callosum the anterior commissure, and particularly the dorsal hippocampal commissure. One of their
findings was that right hemispheric dominance constitute

a major cause for enhanced spirituality in some individuals. In these subjects they tell us, when complex magnetic fields are applied externally for the purpose of simulating neuro-electrophysiological patterns in the brain they elicit paroxysmal electro-encephalographic activity that are concomitant with experiences of a "powerful presence" in special. Although the strengths of these fields are about one micro-Tesla (10 mG) at the level of the skull, they have been calculated to be within the nano-Tesla range at the depths of the cerebral cortices and within the nT to pT range where the hippocampus and amygdala are located. The researchers discovered that these fields can produce electro-encephalographic activity in some subjects, and produce differential amounts of alpha rhythms when preferentially applied over the left or right hemispheres. For the purpose of the experiment the researchers make a distinction between normal belief that is perhaps in the goodness of a certain individual, or that I might have good fortune at the roulette table; from belief in the supernatural. They refer to the latter as exotic beliefs, making it easier for them so be distinguished and isolated for the purpose of study. The composite of these beliefs are classified as part of a subculture at it includes those with an inclination for and a history of sensed presence, verbal meaningfulness, and religious beliefs such as the second coming of Christ, the existence of a devil, and, people must be guided to ensure their spiritual development. Semantic and episodic memory processes were used for the purpose of testing the individuals to discern if beliefs or temporal lobe sensitivity could predict or determine outcomes.    After extensive study and experimentation St. Pierre and Persinger (2006) were able to hypothesize that people with *different* beliefs may be more susceptible to *specific* temporal parameters of the field, analogous to the differential efficacy of medications for subtypes of depression.  This is not unlike the description found in the diagnosis and statistical manual for mental illness or  DSM, in which these beliefs are equated with  form of delusional disorder, particularly of the Grandiose Type. In this disorder the individual experiences inflated worth, inflated power and inflated knowledge often coupled with a special relationship with a deity or famous person.

Despite the fact that the study focused on individuals with an elevated temporal lobe sensitivity finding that they were often more responsive to suggestibility, this fact did not constitute a significant correlate in the report of sensed presences as far as the study was concerned. They recognize that for centuries the sense presence has been associated with creativity, inspiration, mystical states and contacts from other dimensions have been reported in some form or another in nearly every culture that share the planet, but the profound experience reported by their subject has lead them to hypothesize that the brain patterns that produce experiences of gods are reproducible in a controlled experimental setting.

The Bwiti nation and its experiment with Ibogaine represents another clear example of how strong belief may assist in guiding a culture towards an end, or in misleading it depending on who is making the judgment. We learn from Vastag (2005) that in Gabon, the Bwiti religion revolves around "visits to the ancestors" induced by eating root bark from the shrub Tabernanthe iboga, the source of ibogaine. Many patients in the West also report emotionally intense, sometimes frightening visions: scenes from childhood, or past mistakes and regrets replayed and somehow released. Debate rages over whether these experiences are key to ibogaine's anti-addictive potential or simply a psychedelic side effect. Two large religious movements which incorporate the use of vegetable hallucinogens have emerged during the past 150 years, both syncretic of Christianity and both consolidated at the national and ethnic level: the Native American Church of the North American Indians, which uses *peyote (Lophophora williamsii)* and the *Bwiti,* practiced by the people of Fang and other locations of Occidental Equatorial Africa which use the *iboga (Tabernanthe iboga* Baillon, Apocynaceae).

## THE BWITIS AND THEIR SIGNIFICANCE

Bwiti religion is widespread in Gabon, both in the interior of the jungle where it originated and in the capital, Libreville. During the last twenty years, it has crossed its frontiers and reached Cameroon, Congo, Zaire, and Equatorial Guinea. In the latter, the Bwitist community is somewhat clandestine because of the energetic opposition of the Catholic missions. According to the Bwitist genesis, the hallucinogenic properties of the *iboga* were first discovered by the Pygmies in the interior of the jungle. They in turn passed their knowledge on the neighboring people, the Apindji and the Mitsogho, who started the first Bwitist rituals. Later on, this knowledge was passed on to the Fang, the Eshira and other ethnic groups throughout southern Gabon. Within the Fang, the Bwitist movement, due to continuous reform and review of its creed, became more and more distant from other tribal cults, which it in part substituted. In particular, the original Bwiti assumed certain characteristics of another ancestral cult, the Byeri, in whose rituals a different hallucinogen was used, *alan* (plural *melan)*. The Byeri advocated a private cult practiced by the descendants of patrilinear families. At the climax of the initiation ceremony, the initiate, under the influence of a strong dose of the *alan* root (the euphorbiaceous *Alchornea floribunda)* was shown the skulls of his ancestors, and upon seeing these he would be able to communicate with the spirits of the dead. For a long time the Bwiti was considered an ancestral cult and even today, the word Bwiti is translated as "dead" or "ancestor", however, as pointed out by Swiderski (1990-91, vol. II:19), its correct etymology may come from

119

"Mbouiti", the proper name of a group of Pygmies currently oc-
cupying a region between Gabon and Zaire. Originally, the
practice of Bwiti included human sacrifice and ritual anthro-
pophagy. This fact is remembered in the Bwitist myth about the
discovery of the *iboga* and the sacrifice of the first woman who
ingested it, Bandzioku. Soon, however, Bwiti rid itself of such
cruel components and substituted these rituals by sacrificing
chickens. The news about Bwitist human sacrifices dwindled
and there are now a few remaining critics in some sectors of the
Gabonese population, particularly the Catholics who still wage
defamatory campaigns against the Bwitists. To be sure, accusations of criminal sorcery and the so-called diabolic illusions
produced by *iboga* have always been part of the history of Bwiti
from its inception. Subsequently, the persecution carried out by
the missionaries with the approval of the French colonial government was felt by the Bwitist communities particularly during
the years 1920 to 1940. Despite the burning of the temples, persecution and killings of religious leaders the movement continued to grow. Bwiti was and still is a thorn for the Catholic missions and actually Bwiti continues to gain new ground in the
combat for religious territory. Having courageously survived
years of constant persecution, Bwiti has been reformed and contributed to the awakening of a national and anti-colonial con-
science and the birth of the new Gabon Republic. The first president of the newly formed Republic was an initiate in the Bwiti
religion which contributed to its resurfacing and to its growing
acceptance. Today, the Bwiti religion is well accepted by a sector of the governing elite, since it is considered a popular religious movement, which keeps and guarantees tribal values

which are considered fundamental to the spirit of the new republic. Government officials, members of the police and the army are Bwiti initiates and regularly leave the city to participate in the night ceremonies taking place in the neighboring jungle villages. The Bwitists consider themselves Christians. That is, "the real Christians", which is of course a sore point among Catholic missionaries who consider the Bwitists bedevilled, dedicated to Satanic cults, while disregarding the promiscuity among the many Africans who frequent their parishes. Bwitist criticism of Christianity became deeper and more coherent when the expansionism practices replaced past persecution: "The Catholic church is a beautiful theory for Sunday, the *iboga* on the contrary is the practice of everyday living. In church, they speak of God, with *iboga,* you live God" (from words by Nengue Me Ndjoung Isidore, ecumenical Bwitist religious leader, presently Magistrate in the Libreville Supreme Court, quoted in <u>Swiderski 1990-91, vol. I:628</u>). The *iboga* used by the Bwitists during the initiation rites and in their night communal "masses" substitutes the host of the Catholic mass, in practice and in concept, and this substitution is the fuel for the harsh contact between Catholics and Bwitists.

## Internal Structure

Bwiti is a complex religion with a rich mythology, the fruit of an intelligent and secular mix of the afro-tribal values and the catholic biblical figures, and an articulate theology which coherently unites animistic concepts and the characteristics of a Christian god. This syncretic mix is continually evolving; in practice, since its inception Bwiti has never ceased to renew it-

121

self, in its outward form and in its content. The free interpretation of the values expressed by the Bwiti movement has resulted in the creation of many sects, each with its own founding father and its own peculiar relationship with Christianity. The presence of one Bwitist leader with an acute critical mind or with a prophetic/static-like quality is sufficient to bring about a change in the community and a new religious current.

Each Bwitist sect has its own temple, which is distinguished by the diverse decorations on the *akun* or central axis of the temple. The *akun* is covered with symbolic motifs associated with the *axis mundi* or cosmic tree. Regarding content, the Bwitist sects are different from one another, according to the degree to which Christian values have been absorbed. Among members of those sects leaning more toward tribal values, the following is a common proverb: "Baptism and *Iboga* are incompatible", but for members of sects involved with Christianity it is not uncommon that they attend Sunday mass after having participated in the Bwitist mass Saturday night.

The Bwitist communities are "open", that is, their rites are not secret (the real secret is the inability to communicate the experience of initiation) which gives freedom of access to the non-initiates; this can be seen from its proselytism. There is no rivalry among the different sects and there are individuals who have been initiated into two or more sects. The sects consist of groups of 10 to 50 people, usually living in the same village, where the Bwitist temple is symbolically located in one of the most accessible streets. Surrounding the temple (*abeñ*), *iboga* bushes ore cultivated and respected by all.

When no services are being held, the temple is used as a place for social gathering, a place for meeting and talking, a space that offers protection. The temple also serves as control center since from its interior one has visual control of the village. The *abeñ* is an ample hut, with wooden wails and roof, consisting of two principal rooms, the ceremonial room and the "sacristy". The entire structure resembles the structure of a human body, the pale supporting the roof is the spinal cord, the ceremonial room is the body, the "tomb" seen at the end of the ceremonial is similar to an altar, and the site for the musicians is considered its heart, the *akun* is its penis, the sacristy is its head and the two doors opening to the ceremonial room are its ears. In the interior of the sacristy, a sort of niche built in the manner of a tabernacle contains the powdered root of the *iboga* and the ceremonial spoons used to administer it.

In each community members are divided between the simple initiates (*bandzi*) and the "officiating" members of different gradations. The term officiating is given following a learning period and superior initiations. During the ceremonies, each officiating member has a precise role; at the very top of the community is the *nima,* the religious leader, followed by the *yemba,* an officiating member who comments on the rituals being followed during the ceremony. Then, follows the guardian of the temple and the tabernacle, then the dance director and the musicians among which the harpist has a special function. Together with these mostly male officiating members is found the woman responsible for female affairs (woman are the majority in most Bwitist communities). All the officiating members of the cult live like the rest of the village and are usually married. (Among the Fang, male polygamy is prevalent).

## The Initiation Rite

The cycle of rituals of all Bwitist sects is based on a religious calendar similar to the Catholic one. The main difference being that the Bwitist rites are conducted at night, as are most rituals connected with the use of hallucinogens. The members of the community get together at night from Saturday to Sunday, and at Christmas and Easter time, at which times they partake of the *iboga* (*ngozé*) as communion. Apart from those times when they all get together, the individual initiation rite is experienced by those desiring to join the community and it consists primarily of the ingestion of a large dose of *iboga,* much larger than when taken during the normal *ngozé*. This factor takes the initiate to an altered state of consciousness, to static-mystical states, to a direct contact with the sacred. The occurrence of such initiation leads us to consider Bwiti as a *complete* psychedelic religion, that is, having an initiating impact which results in great alteration of the individual's consciousness. Among the Bwitist the moment of initiation is the moment of greatest illumination and must be taken into consideration for the rest of the initiates' life: in each moment of crisis, the Bwitist goes back to the time of initiation, thus putting himself at the best strategic point of observation. At the initiation rite, the ingestion of the hallucinogen is preceded by an offering to the jungle and its trees, and a confession in front of the officiating members and a ritual bath. The confession covers all past life. The omission of sins may result in a "bad trip" with disastrous consequences and even permanent madness, and should the omitted sin be related to homicide, the death of the initiate will ensue.

The effects of the massive dose of *iboga* (a few hectograms of the powdered root) which the initiate must ingest little by little during 7 to 12 hours, last three consecutive days and nights. During this time the initiate will remain lying down on the floor of the sacristy, assisted by a couple considered as the "father" and "mother" of the initiation process. Besides the "parents" other members of the community are present, they will accompany their future brother in his long journey to the sounds of the harp or in silence. Any of the present members may ingest *iboga* during these nights: a companion during the "great journey" also experiencing the effects. The initiate's consciousness will undergo changes more and more intense, becoming more separated from his surrounding reality until he loses touch. At this time, usually during the third night, an officiating member will pinch the initiate with a thorn to ensure his separateness with exterior world. If he does not react, it is understood that he is undergoing the climax of the experience. The moment is acknowledged in western terminology using the term beatific vision or *epopteia*. This moment is referred to by all Bwitists so "baptized" as going to the root of life itself and direct dialogue with god. During the vision, the initiate undertakes long journeys to the land of the dead, who serve as mediators with the divine. He may also encounter his ancestors or other persons known to him. Others find celestial figures during their journey, the Virgin Mary, Jesus Christ, St. Peter, shedding their divine light. Others have direct encounters with God. The hallu-cinations experienced during the trip are full of profound sym-bolic meaning, personal as well as cultural; the world of the jungle with its trees, plants, and animals acts as an experimental and imaginative substrate for the visions. Always during the vision, the spirits of the dead, Jesus Christ or any other entity tells the initiate his new name, the initiatory name (*nkombo*), a name that is added to the initiate's proper names. As an ecstatic religion, the Bwiti relies on the hallucinogen and the subsequent personal psychic experience to duly introduce its doctrine. It is the initiatory experience which brings about an act of faith, an act which follows the moment of illumination; this act of faith in Christianity always must precede any show of conviction: "il faut voir pour croire" ("one must see to believe") is a common proverb in all Bwitist sects, in polemic contrast to "it is enough to believe" as the Catholic mission preach. Bwiti is a "reveal-ing" religion, that is, it constantly reveals: it reveals itself to the individual during each initiation. Following the three days and nights of the initiation, the initiate wakes up to what he consid-ers a new life. Sometimes energetic intervention on the part of the officiating member is necessary to wake up the initiate and at times, the loss of consciousness may continue into the fol-lowing days. This is interpreted as a positive sign since it is tak-en to be contact with the divine. Only on rare occasions, has the initiate failed to wake up and died. As in the rare instance of a "bad trip", *iboga* is not considered the cause; it is the individual who is responsible, because of his impurity and bad thoughts. Upon awakening, the individual relates his experience to the community, and others have the opportunity to corroborate their visions. After this, he is considered a *bandzi* in every regard. A long sleep which may last days concludes the rite of initiation. This *iboga* baptism may be experienced at any age, as is the Catholic baptism. Currently, in some sects there is a tendency to initiate relatives, especially their children, from ages 8 to 10, which is followed by a second initiation as adults. The great freedom of interpretation of the Bwitist canon allows for big changes in the modalities of the initiation.

## RELIGION IN HUMAN RELATION

The task of exploring the role of religion in human progress or non-progress is a rather difficult one, one that requires an overwhelming degree of what is referred to as intellectual honesty, that is, a willingness to explore areas that are considered off limits to most humans, and confront what are considered established norms. Because of that, realistic research on a subject such as religion is all the more challenging and for it we must thank the few daring researchers, who risk so much to stare down and confront established norms. Old friends for daring to challenge the sacred have cast many off as pariahs and others were shunned by colleagues and other professionals, as they embarked on a subject matter that made them uneasy. To add to that, the few who would in the past dare to venture into these delicate areas would often do so denouncing the established order as well as its administrators, by-passing the critical mass of thinkers required to have some impact on the subject. This denunciation and open confrontation has led to confusion rather than clarity, particularly for those tapped under the influence of a rather powerful socio-political infrastructure. The result of this of course, is limited research material on a subject of this nature. There are researchers and academicians dedicated to this subject but their numbers are limited, and since the first label attached to anyone who dares to take on this subject is that of atheist, there is a considerable reduction in the pool of intellectuals willing to go that far.

No other generation in the past has had this much exposure to scientific facts and evidence surrounding the presence of humans in this universe. If for no other reason than that, we owe it to ourselves to persuade black families of all religious inclination or none at all, to guarantee that these facts are not hidden from their children.

Mannings (2004) argues this, based on the principle that increased understanding and access to truth will always benefit mankind. The methodical and tenacious pursuit of hidden knowledge and its subsequent translation into common language is an enterprise that should be honored, encouraged, and applauded. Seen in this light rational truth becomes a bridge over the chasm of ignorance and superstition, a connection between the known and the unknown, but unfortunately far too many choose to withdraw to familiar territory rather than risk the personal challenge of discovery that accompanies the genuine quest for truth (p. xv).

Manning (2004) offers a fair and balanced analysis as he plunges head on into the subject with an  introduction of the term "psycho-spirituality," with a warning that it is not yet a part of the English dictionary and the reason he gives for this, is that the concept of the psyche and the spirit are considered to relate to the psychological mind and the religious soul respectively (p. 81). As such, they are rarely used collaboratively in the same context due to the long established reticence of psychologists and religionists to enter each other's domain in anything but a critical role. The psycho-spiritual theory may be best understood as an inclusive conceptual framework within which competing theories may find a place of union. A framework however, with built in empirical filters that only allow for self-evident truth to pass (p 90).

Manning (2004) then points to the "True Religious Experience" holding it as partly responsible for the endless confusion around the subject of religion, adding that it is hidden like the proverbial pearl of great price among the muck and grime of so much human ambition, ignorance, and dysfunction within institutionalized religion. That even after science has evaluated all the possible psychological motivation for religious practice there will still remain this unfathomable dimension to religion known as The Religious Experience or TRE. It operates under a different set of rules, and is depicted by many as an enlightening flow of wisdom, peace and universal cognition, described often as ecstatic, mystical, spiritual or transcendental. It is depicted in various faith traditions the genuine religious encounter is experienced as an uplifting numinous event, one in which subjectivity and objectivity are indistinguishable. One in which the individual mind, psyche or spirit merges with that of the universe, at least in theory, if only for a moment or two. Such is the reported essence of the genuine religious experience a phenomenon which while differing across the board in specific interpretation is nevertheless universally consistent in many other ways (p. 41).

Manning (2004) also inform us that in an effort to understand the phenomenon during their times Freud and Jung brought the psychological mechanism of the religious journey slowly into focus, discussing the concept of god spirituality and the soul the mind and religion in such terms as the numinous realm and the unconscious, the individual subconscious, archetypes, the animus and anima, complexes and neuroses etc, thus introducing a new scientific lexicon to traditionally spiritual matters. Having been reasonably settled in their respective fields for over a century, this invasion by psychologist into sacrosanct religious territory caused ripples of disturbance on both sides of the divide, in short an uneasy truce had been violated (pp. 79).

Manning (2004), points to the endless confusion that pervades the religious realm and cites as an example the absolute lack of agreement among believers in the meaning given to the words that describes their belief system. Manning (2004) notes that from the outset that there are a great many ongoing debates within the various faith traditions as well as within the discipline of psychology regarding the nature and meaning of overlapping terms such as mind, spirit, heart, soul and spirituality. These terms though nebulous in nature and technically imprecise in their description, both scientists and theologians

131

acknowledge the existence of a real beyond the conscious. Manning (2004) then offers a personal testament based on many years of interreligious and interdenominational inter- actions that found that there is hardly a theologian or a cleric who possess a comprehensive literal grasp of the meaning of such terms (spiritual, mind, soul etc). Evidence of this is an interview conducted with a dozen attendees to a religious conference, all of whom were from religious sectors of the Christian religion i.e. Roman Catholics, Sev- enth Day Adventists, Christian Fundamentalists, Mormons, Unificationists, and Jehovah Witnesses. They were each asked to list three words or a short phrase to define each of the following words: god, heaven, hell, spirit or soul, pray- er, religion and spirituality. There was hardly an instance where two people in any particular denomination group listed the same properties or definitions even for any one item on the list, and on several cases none of the answers matched at all thereby accumulating so many abstract ad- jectives, nouns and concepts as to render the subject under discussion practically meaningless (p. xvii).

Despite the cautionary admonition of true saints and sages and the bloody evidence of religious history, in our ignorant and foolhardy certainties we nonetheless continue to accept systematic, absolutist and specious religious be- liefs that all but prevent the novel discovery of truth. Symptomatic of mass neurosis, and undoubtedly linked to our abovementioned need to submit to something greater

132

than ourselves, such intransigent religious attitudes are indeed the root cause of the problem. Indeed the most disturbing aspect of such popular religions is not so much the fact that it facilitates mass neurosis, but that it insidiously presupposes to deny the facts, choosing instead to present itself as the preeminent healthy feature of society—a blatant lie whose prolongation and support is patently dependent on the ignorance and on the neurotic delusion of its adherents. Cleverly, through the systematic indoctrination and the psychological manipulation of the young and the unlearned, in combination with a strategy of suppression, denial and censorship of scientific evidence, many profoundly irrational religious beliefs have become so rooted in the collective psyche that it is now difficult to know where reality ends and mythology begins even in our ultramodern cultures. In their desperate dash to defend questionable beliefs many otherwise mentally healthy individuals have become unwitting psycho-spiritual casualties of the operational policies of religious institutions whose corporate interests are manifestly tied to the systematic and unscrupulous propagation of implausible and often delusional doctrines. Manning (2004) explains that when speaking in general of traditional, institutionalized religions vs. specific exceptions to the rule, the true or psycho spiritual education development or empowerment of the individuals has long since been supplanted by corporate goals and objectives, and by the unscrupulous manipulation of self-absorbed ecclesiasts (p. 183).

On the subject of mental disturbances and religion, Manning (2004) points to Rokeach's (1960) findings regarding the general state of mind of most religious people in that it contradicts the long held notion that religious people enjoy greater peace of mind than non-believers. Rokeach's (1960) argued that believers complain more often working under great tension, sleeping fitfully and other like symptoms pointing to a test designed to measure manifest anxiety, believers generally scored higher than non-believers. Manning (2004) argues that this anxiety is linked to the authoritarian construct which continue to promote the concept of individual worthlessness, and that disempowered and disenfranchised by such morbid beliefs religionists exist in a subliminal state of anxiety and addiction (p. 9). This, claims Manning (2004), fuels the development of a debilitating neurosis, one that keeps them living in fear, not love; and whether they are consciously aware of it the god they mold from this sense of fear can do no other than continue to feed their neurosis. Ritualizing those neurosis into acceptable social norms in the form of religious belief religious and religious practices may serve to temporarily contain the problem at the individual level, but in the long run the individual neurosis can only suffer its own existence by coagulating into a socially acceptable collective form which is the church, and in doing so, provide the adherents with a perceived sense of security and a false sense of mental and emotional wel-lbeing. Through the agency of authoritarian or exclusive religious belief, the individual neurosis is thus fuelled, sanctified, justified, and ultimately transformed into a collective psychosis. Dogmatic convictions soon replace healthy questions with false absolutes. Manning (2004) then quotes the American psychiatrist Thomas Szasz with the following:" Doubt is to certainty as neurosis is to psychosis. The neurotic is in doubt and has fears about persons and things; the psychotic has convictions and makes claims about them. In short, the neurotic has problems, the psychotic has solutions" (p.10).

Manning (2004) argues that in the case of the obsessive religionists suffering from paranoia or delusion and often both, the presence of holy terminology and rituals sur-rounding their particular obsession or addiction not only allows the afflicted adherent to reside n a state of denial of their condition, but what is far worse actually gives them license to play out their religious superiority complexes with devastating results in society. That as the lines be-tween reality and delusion are blurred God and Truth are reduced to mere subjective justifications for all manners of evil, and our ethical and moral responsibilities to each oth-er are displaced (p. 11).

Manning (2004) then introduces Erich Fromm's as-sessment of the role of psychoanalysis in relation to  reli-gious delusion with the following quote: "to help man dis-cern truth from falsehood in himself is the basic aim of psychoanalysis (p. 10). Manning (2004), comments that for the most part modern religious beliefs are no more than institutionalized products of our collective fears, tinged with nostalgia and romantic myths, and endorsed by long standing traditions generation after generation. But fear remains the overwhelming variable, fear of the devil, fear of hell, fear of sin, fear of evil and fear of anything that is not of our own persuasion. Ultimately, Manning (2004) tells us, we are simply reflecting our own fear of ourselves, of a terrible and incomprehensible god and of the mysterious universe that surrounds us, and that religion conveniently provides the locus and the symbol forms that justify these fears (p. 11). Manning (2004) saved the best of his analysis for sectarianism, referring to it as the most sinister of religious contradictions and responsible for spawning all manners of neurotic and psychotic manipulations, social dysfunctions, enmity, violence, and institutionalized corruption. Manning (2004) arrives at the conclusion that sectarianism is an offense against the very soul and mind of mankind as well as the concept of the universal family, blocking true growth, knowledge, and understanding (p. xv).

Manning (2004) brings us to Erich Fromm once more, this time with Fromm's full description of humanistic religion. Fromm argues that:

> Humanistic religion is centered around man and his strengths. Man must develop the poser of reason in

order to understand himself, to his relationship to his fellow men and his position in the universe. He must recognize the truth, both with regard to his limitations and his potentialities. He must develop his powers of love for others as well as for himself and experience the solidarity of all living beings. He must have principles and norms to guide him in his aim. Religious experience in this kind of religion is the experience of the All, based on one's relatedness to the world as it is grasped with thought and with love. Man's aim in humanistic religion is to achieve the greatest strength not the greatest powerlessness; virtue is self-realization, not obedience. Faith is certainty of conviction based upon one's experience of thought and feeling...God is a symbol of man's own powers ...and not the symbol of force and domination (p. 27).

The world has witnessed the rise of despots, genocidal mass murderers of every hue, of ever complexions and of nearly every religion, and it has come to the conclusion that what nearly all of these individuals have in common is a loveless, neglected and abused childhood. Miller (2010) offers a comprehensive analysis on this subject with what are quite possibly two of history's most cruel despots Adolf Hitler and Joseph Stalin. Miller (2010) argues against the notion that genetics plays a role in the creation of individuals who are depraved and criminal by nature.

Miller (2010), commented that she is yet to come across such an individual, and that the childhood biographies of dictators and serial killers that she has studied show them without exception to have been the victims of extreme cruelty. She then points to the case of Germany stating that taken to its logical conclusion, genetic theory ought to be able to explain why thirty years before the advent of the Third Reich, Germany should have brought forth millions of children whose genetics make up was so badly contaminated that in adulthood they were willing to hand themselves to Hitler's atrocities without turning a hair. Miller (2010), then poses the question as to why there had not been such an accumulation of rogue genes in Germany either before or since that period, and the answer offered was that Hitler and his cohorts were part of a generation of children who had been exposed to brutal physical correction and humiliation, and who later vented their pent-up feeling of anger and helpless rage on innocent victims. Safe in the knowledge that they were doing so with the Fuhrer's blessings, they were finally able to give free reign to those feelings without fear of punishment. In short Miller (2010), claims, wherever cruelty and humiliation are a part of parenting those methods will be faithfully reflected in the behavior of young people as they deny the pain of the humiliation they've been through selecting convenient scapegoats as they advance their harebrained ideological justification for their depredations (p. 50). Miller (2010), states that in the name of good parenting millions of children all over the world are subjected to some of the worst form of terrorism. The child standing helpless, speechless, and trembling before the unpredictable, incomprehensible, brutal and indiscriminate violence of their parents who are in effect unconsciously avenging themselves for the suffering in their own childhood; suffering they never came to terms with since they have never admitted to its existence. Mao Tse Tung was the son a strict teacher who set out to drum obedience and wisdom into him with the aid of severe physical correction. The world was later to discover what wisdom Mao later attempted to install in his country at the cost of more than thirty five million lives (p. 69). Miller (2010) discovered in her research that like *Hitler, Joseph Stalin* was exposed to incredible brutality as a child and had no helping witness to turn to. He had no idea that it was his bodily memory that drove him to act out his private history of unremitting childhood distress on the colossal stage afforded him by the immensity of the Soviet Union. Joseph Stalin's brutal treatment at the hands of an alcoholic father made his life a living inferno, with the dread of being killed at any moment by this unpredictable maniac. As an adult, he had to power to fend off that fear by humiliating others (p. 68).

Recognition of these facts may be helpful in improving our own thinking and our ability to analyze our reality correctly, following the trail of our research to where it takes us may not be the easiest thing to do but it may be bordering on the inevitable.  The blending of cultures the respect for differences and the need for greater peace and tranquility demands an honest reckoning with all the difficult subject matters we try so hard to evade.

The greatest challenge remains, our ability to keep our hands off the coming generations, both figuratively and literally, allowing them the right to be different, and to question all that we heretofore have taken as a given and have accepted  as gospel.

# RELIGIOUS INDOCTRINATION AND THE AFRICAN AMERICAN FAMILY

Nowhere is the force of religious indoctrination as palpable as when it relates to impressionable minds, minds yet under formation and testing the boundaries of their immediate environment. The potentials they embody and the promise these new minds hold for the future of humanity is incalculable, yet too often it is here that the rest of the society finds it convenient to entrap these minds, fill them with the very fears and prejudices forced on them a few short decades earlier, thus completing the endless cycle of confusion and haplessness that has come to define what we know today as civilization. The courage to end this cycle and allow children to think for themselves and develop their own concepts of the world they now inherit is our greatest challenge. The urge to impose our own prejudices on new generations of humans is almost irresistible to adults, and aided by the clergy, the village priests, the sorcerers or the magician's ineloquent parents often succeed at obtaining the alliance of their children to the views of the world they themselves hold. The few children with the courage to resist are considered rebels, or discontents lacking in gratitude for all that has been done for them. The nonconformist rendered confused and full of self-doubt, not knowing where to turn for support or what fate awaits him or her as they strike out on their own in a world structured only according to well demarcated lines of religious bias and religious prejudices that surfaces almost unconsciously in those they happen to come across. The open-minded child or adolescent in search of real answers is often lost among a multitude of bobbing heads and conformists urging them to tow the line and go along with whatever dogma that happens to be dominant in their immediate environment. This book explores the impact of religious indoctrination on the African American family and on the African American culture as a whole. Special attention will be paid to the ways in which dogma affects overall human growth, emotional stability and the intellectual development of those who define themselves as religious. The institution of slavery will be explored extensively with great emphasis placed on the extent to which this institution may have served as a convenient vehicle for imposing a foreign dogma and a foreign thought process on an otherwise peaceful and submissive population. The paper will also explore whether the institution of slavery could have survived as long as it did without the skillful application of religious indoctrination, and it will conclude with a sober assessment of the current state of mind of the ex-slaves and their determination to command the respect of the people of the world.

The research will be guided by the thoughts and expres

sions of some of the more outstanding African American

and Caribbean intellectual leaders as it relates to this subject, thinkers like Frederick Douglass, Carter G. Woodson, W.E.B. Du Bois, Booker T. Washington and others. These views will be explored extensively, particularly as they relate to education, and how the administering of education to African Americans may have affected their drive for economic parity, and their demands for greater respect within and outside of their geographic borders. No group serves better as an example of a group disproportionately affected by some if not all of the complexities mentioned earlier, in part because they have so little to do with their own predicament in the west.

The African presence in the Americas, particularly in the United States of North America, has been a unique experience, something unprecedented as far as we know. In history there has never been a case of a people so completely transformed by their captors. Bradley and Cartledge (2011) argue that if a single origin for the practice and maintenance of chattel slavery in antiquity can be identified, it would likely have a lot to do with the rights of victors in warfare (p.2). In these cases they often found it feasible to be benevolent with the population and establish with them some sense of partnership or collaboration. Never before was there an attempt to completely destroy a people who for all intent and purposes were neither hostile nor threatening to the dominant group. This group that constituted the most recent subjects of institutionalized

143

slaves were degraded, humiliated and totally dehumanized, for reasons that even today are still hard to comprehend. It should have been obvious from the outset that reducing a people to the level of lower animals and excluding them from the process of human growth and development would have benefitted no one, yet, that systematic process was carried out if for no other reason than perhaps to eradicate any thought of independence and self-sufficiency. Other than the immediate and very temporary profit of very few, it is hard to imagine what other purpose there might be for such a policy. Five centuries later the victims of this historic atrocity, the ex-slaves, are still attempting to understand their predicament and to produce remedies to their adverse conditions.

Despite the massive and elaborate effort to dehumanize, degrade and humiliate the slaves, several among them have emerged with extraordinary intellect, the kind of intellect that can not only lead their people out of poverty and ignorance but also rather provide the much-needed leadership the world so desperately needs. Some of the most outstanding among those leaders to name a few were, Carter G. Woodson, W.E. B. Du Bois, and Booker T. Washington all educators and contemporaries of each other. Despite the fact that it is not a psychological treatise, Woodson (1933) deals a extensively with the state of mind of African Americans of the nineteenth and twentieth century, first stating that: "The large majority of the Negroes who have put on the finishing touches of our best colleges are all but worthless in the development of their people" (p. 24). Woodson (1933) is very critical of religious dogma and indoctrination particularly as the subject impacts the lives of African Americans, commenting that, "In schools of theology Negroes are taught the interpretation of the bible worked out by those who have justified segregation and winked at the economic debasement of the Negro sometimes almost to the point of starvation" (p. 25). To this comment Woodson (1933) adds his analysis of the problems surrounding the Black preachers and their flock, stating:

> The people have never been taught what religion [really] is, for most of the preachers find it easier to stimulate the superstition which develops in the unenlightened mind. Religion in such hands, then becomes something with which you take advantage of weak people. Why try to enlighten the people in such matters when superstition serves just as well for exploitation (p. 106).

Woodson (1933) avoids the usual ranting and raving about racism and oppression although he recognizes its ever presence, he held Black responsible for themselves and their destiny while pointing to the devices in place to make their lives even more difficult. level some criticism against theology schools: as in this instance: In geography the races were described in conformity with the program of usual propaganda to engender in whites a race hate of the Negroes, and in the Negroes' contempt for themselves (p. 32). Woodson (1933) goes on to say, "Looking over the courses of study of the public schools one finds little to show that the Negro figures in these curricula. In supplementary matters, a good deal of some Negro is occasionally referred to, but oftener the race is mentioned only to be held up to ridicule" (p. 99). Despite his recognized brilliance and wealth of knowledge on matters concerning the African American reality of his time, Woodson was still limited on matters related to the real history of Africa. We find elements of this limitation when he refers to Africa as being a contributor to world civilization: "Africa according to recent discoveries, has contributed as much to the progress of mankind as Europe has, and the early civilization of the Mediterranean world was decidedly influenced by Africa" (p. 100). Woodson (1933) further added that the empires of Egypt, Ethiopia, Mali and Songhai in addition to other cultures in the African interior, were equal or greater in stature to that of Mesopotamia, Greece or Rome" (110). This is evidence of the massive negative propaganda that remained in force through the time of the writing and publishing of his masterpiece since the archeologists and researchers of the eighteenth and nineteenth century like Jean-François Champollion (French, 1790–1832) and others who were already aware, not just of the African contribution to world civilization but that Africa in fact gave the world its civilization. The expressions, "cradle of civilization and birthplace of the human race" which became popular since the consciousness movement of the sixties, had not yet been connected to the name, Africa. To his credit however, Woodson (1933) later added this on the subject, "Thinkers are now saying that the early cultures of the Mediterranean were chiefly African. Such has been the education of the Negro, they have been taught facts of history but they have never learned how to think" (p. 101). The imitation of others, as the Negro does, Woodson (1933) argues, is not flattery but a misguided approach to be caught up with the rest of the world. The argument they present often is that what others have done we can do, which on face value is a good argument, but in scratching the surface we realize that what others have done we may not need to do. In this particular respect the Negro education can be seen as a failure, and disastrously do, since the race is especially in need of vision and invention to give humanity something new (p.101). Demonstrating once more his inclination to a more analytical and scholarly approach Woodson (1933) suggests: "In our schools, and especially in schools of religion, attention should be given to the study of the Negro as he developed during the antebellum period by showing to what extent that remote culture was determined by ideas which the Negro brought with him from Africa. To take it for granted that the antebellum Negro was an ignoramus or that the native brought from

Africa had not a valuable culture, merely because some prejudice writer had said so, does not show the attitude of scholarship, and the Negro student who direct their courses accordingly will never be able to grapple with the social problems presented today by the church (p. 106). In speaking to their miss-education, Woodson (1933) was not just referring to what the so-called educated Negro was taught in schools by the Caucasians, but also the irrational and self-defeating concepts they held of themselves, something that may have had its genesis even prior to his captivity and subsequent enslavement.

Woodson (1933), draws attention to the lack of confidence the Negro has in himself as the primary thing that has kept him down, adding that if the Negro would be as fair to his own as he has been to others, this would be all that is necessary to give him a new lease on life and start the upright trend. However, the program for the uplift of the Negro in this country must be based on a scientific study of the Negro from within, to develop in him the power to do for himself what his oppressor will never do to elevate him to the level of others (p. 84). Woodson (1933) saves his most scathing criticism for the Negro church, commenting on the unfortunate fact that it does not conceive of social uplift as part of its duties, and he concludes this commentary by stating that in the church where the Negro enjoys the greatest freedom and independence, efforts must be made to get rid of the preachers who are not prepared to help the people advance. Those who keep the people in ignorance and play upon their emotions must be exiled (pp. 62,106).

The sobering and uplifting analysis of Carter Goodwin Woodson is matched only by the passion and eloquence of another African American giant, Frederick Douglass.

It takes a Douglass scholar to fully comprehend the panoply of forces Douglass was up against during his life-time. Born in the north, (eastern shores of the state Mary-land) in 1818, reportedly of a white father and Black slave mother, Douglass' circumstances were unusual in relation to that of other slaves. In his autobiography, he reports a loving and devoted mother who risked unspeakable torture the few occasions she had to walk twelve miles in the dead of night just to lay eyes on him. The treasure of those mo-ments may well have been the foundation of Douglass' re-solved commitment to ending slavery and uplifting his fel-low humans. Scholars of African American history identify Frederick Douglass through his famous Fourth of July speech, delivered in Rochester, New York, on that date in the year eighteen hundred and fifty two. Excerpts of the speech are included only for the purpose of illustration, and bringing samples of Douglass' eloquence to a genera-tion that seldom ventures this far in their inquiry:

Fellow citizens, pardon me, allow me to ask, why am I called upon to speak here today? What have I, or those I represent, to do with your national independence? Are the great principles of political freedom and of natural justice, embodied in that Declaration of Independence, extended to us? and am I, therefore, called upon to bring our humble offering to the national altar, and to confess the benefits and express devout gratitude for the blessings resulting from your independence to us? What, to the American slave, is your Fourth of July? I answer: a day that reveals to him, more than all other days in the year, the gross injustice and cruelty to which he is the constant victim. To him, your celebration is a sham; your boasted liberty, an unholy license; your national greatness, swelling vanity; your boasted liberty, an unholy license; your national greatness, swelling vanity; your sounds of rejoicing are empty and heartless; your denunciation of tyrants, brass-fronted impudence; your shouts of liberty and equality, hollow mockery; your prayers and hymns, your sermons and thanksgivings, with all your religious parade and solemnity, are, to him, more bombast, fraud, deception, impiety, and hypocrisy-a thin veil to cover up crimes which would disgrace a nation of savages (freemaninstitute.org). Douglass was hailed by Blacks and Whites alike despite these strong words. This, I believe, is testimony to the greatness of his character.

Born Frederick Augustus Washington Bailey in 1818, on Holmes Hill farm in Talbot County, on the Eastern Shore of Maryland, to Harriet Bailey, a slave, Frederick never knew his father but suspected him to be his owner,

Captain Aaron Anthony. Young Frederick was sent to live with the Hugh Auld family in Baltimore when he was only seven years old in 1826. There he taught himself to read and write after some initial lessons from his master's wife. In 1834 Frederick was hired out to Edward Covey, a "slave breaker", to break his spirit and make him accept his condition as a slave. Two years into the ordeal young Frederick now eighteen attempted to escape but his plot was discovered. While working in the Baltimore shipyards as a caulker young Frederick meets and falls in love with Anna Murray, a free Negro (daughter of slaves). With Anna's assistance, Frederick escapes slavery in 1838 and goes to New York City where he marries Anna Murray. Under constant threats of being returned to his master, Frederick and his wife Anna moved to New Bedford, Massachusetts settling under the new name Frederick Douglass. In 1839 the twenty one year old Douglass was hired by the abolitionist William Lloyd Garrison as a lecturer for the American Anti-Slavery Society spending the next four years on the lecture circuit speaking out against slavery and campaigning for rights of free Blacks. Douglass made his first trip to England after the publication of his first autobiography in 1845 at age twenty-seven. The popularity of the book renewed calls for his recapture and return to Baltimore, so Douglass sought refuge with his abolitionist friends in England who subsequently purchased his freedom from his former master Hugh Auld, for the sum of

£159. When he returned to the United States in 1847 Douglass relocated to Rochester N.Y. from where he published The North Star, which was to later morph into *the Frederick Douglass' Paper* and subsequently *Douglass' Monthly*.

In 1859 Douglass was forced to call on his British friends once more when he became implicated in his friend John Brown's efforts to begin a slave insurrection with an attack on Harper's Ferry. John Brown stayed at the Douglass' a year earlier where together they worked on plans for a slave insurrection, but Douglass later advised John Brown against the raid referring to it as suicidal. When Brown and his men were captured Douglass was sure that the authorities would be coming after him so he made his way to Canada, sailing to England off the Canadian coast. Douglass returned to the United States in 1860 upon the death of his eleven year old daughter Annie but was not charged with any connection with the raid. This was the year prior to the beginning of the civil war and Douglass was able to persuade Lincoln to establish a Negro regiments in the Union Army, one in which Douglass and his three sons Lewis, Charles and Frederick Jr. were able play a significant role (p. 788 )

Douglass embraced every opportunity to denounce the hypocrisy surrounding the ideals of a new nation with its declaration of independence and that new nation's willingness to degrade other human beings. Such discrepancy could not sit well with Douglass, and he had great difficulty putting it to rest. Colaiaco (2006) reminds us:

> Frederick Douglass awakened the conscience of the nation, compelling Americans to confront the greatest moral dilemma in its history. His attack on slavery and defense of human dignity brought him into conflict with the slave states of the South and with the states of the North, where free blacks were segregated and deprived of the full benefits of citizenship. He confronted a nation reluctant to take the necessary steps to abolish slavery. Despite formidable obstacles, he refused to be silenced. Delivering hundreds of speeches on behalf of those condemned to live in slavery, Douglass inspired, converted, and provoked. He mesmerized his audiences. No speaker was more impassioned, more devoted to the advancement of human rights. No person understood better the meaning of the American creed as embodied in the Declaration of Independence and the Preamble to the United States Constitution, and no one was more eloquent in summoning the nation to fulfill this creed for all, regardless of race (p. 6).

It may be said that nothing infuriated Douglass more than the Missouri Compromise of 1850 for not only did it create the possibility of extending slavery to the newly conquered territories, it created a new Fugitive Slave law, one that made life impossible even for those slaves that had escaped to the Northern territories several years earlier. In other words, the law was retroactive and stronger than one enacted in 1793. Colaiaco (2006) reports:

> An infuriated Douglass lashed out against the insidious prospect of extending slavery in the territories on the basis that it is a right. He added that the impudence of slaveholders exceeds everything! They talk about the right (!!) of slavery, just as if it were possible for slavery to have rights. The right to introduce it into the territories!...Slavery has no RIGHTS. It is a foul and damning outrage upon all rights, and has no rights to exist anywhere, in our out of the territories (p.66).

Harriet Beecher Stowe the acclaimed author of the novel Uncle Tom's Cabin, was an admirer of Douglass and referred to him as the hammer blow against slavery, and published her novel in book form the same year Douglass delivered his famous Fourth of July speech. In it he argued that: slavery has been nationalized in its most horrible and revolting form, New York had become Virginia and the power to hunt, hold and sell men women and children as slaves was no longer just a matter of individual states, it was now the law of the land in its entirety.

Douglass commended the church of England for its anti-slavery stance, and for its role in abolishing slavery from all British territories in 1833. Douglass then rebuked the American churches for their hypocrisy as it remained indifferent to the evils of slavery, and in many cases siding with oppression. He accused them of shamelessly giving the sanction of religion and the bible to the whole system of slavery, finding in those ancient writings endorsement for the institution in arguments that supports the relationship between slaves and their masters as something ordained by God. In his vehemence, Douglass declared that he welcomed infidelity, atheism or anything else in preference to that gospel (p.70).

In all of his denunciation of slavery, Douglass supported his arguments with the words of that sacred document known as the Constitution of the United States of America. What he could not reconcile however was the clause in that document that denied the status of humanity to one seventh of its population only because of their pigmentation. This clause was the three-fifths clause, and the efforts to understand its reason for being a part of the constitution, made a genuine constitutional scholar out of Douglass.

Colaiaco (2006) tells us that for years Douglass concurred with his friend William Lloyd Garrison that the constitution supported slavery. This point was emphasized by Wendell Phillips a leading Garrisonian who pointed to the three-fifths compromise in Article 1, section 2. James Madison's records of the 1787 of the Constitutional Convention debate, made public only after his death in 1840, revealed that there was extensive debate over slavery but that the term itself never made it into the document. Instead of slaves and slavery words like "other persons", "such persons", and "persons held to servitude or labor." In fact, Colaiaco (2006) reveals, "one could not tell from the explicit language of the original Constitution that slavery existed in the United States of America prior to the Civil War, that the word slavery did not expressly enter the constitution until the Thirteenth Amendment was signed into law. The constitutional scholar in Douglass convinced him that if the framers intended to establish slavery as the law of the land they would have spelled it out in the constitution (p. 74). Colaiaco (2006) tells us that Douglass defended the principles in the constitution from any person or branch of government that attempted to trample it for their own advantages, arguing that the Supreme Court deviated from the ideals of the Founders each time a compromise with slavery was made. Douglass was confident that if the people were to read the document for themselves they would find that nowhere does the Constitution explicitly recognize slavery as a legitimate part of American society.

What was revealed in this research is that among the framers of the constitution, the founding fathers, as they are often referred to, were many opponents of slavery, this factor has made it now possible to understand the reason for the complex concept of the three-fifths of a person.

We learn, again from Colaiaco (2006) that the concept was introduced officially in the 1787 Constitutional Convention debate over political representation. The delegates had agreed upon a bicameral Congress, with proportional representation in the House of Representatives. But the southern delegates made it clear that they would reject a Union that did not include slavery. They desired a Constitution that supported the right to own slaves. On the question of representation in the Senate, the convention agreed that each state, regardless of size, would have two Senators. The question of the senate was already settled but the house was a more complex matter. Since representation in the House would be determined by population, the Convention had to consider the question of who should be counted. The South, wishing to increase its electoral power in the House of Representatives, wanted to count slaves as whole people. Holding greater numbers, the South would be able to protect the system of slavery. If all slaves were included in the population count, the South would have had 50 percent of the seats in the House. Regarding human bondage as a blatant contradiction to the equality principle of the Declaration of Independence, most northern delegates believed that the Constitution should not endorse slavery. They wanted no slaves to be counted, thus granting them greater voting power to control Congress. If no slaves were included in the population count, the South would have had only 41 percent of the seats in the House. Northern delegates also realized that allowing the South to count Slaves for purposes of representation would provide an incentive to increase the slave population and this was an undesirable prospect.

After more than a month of vigorous debate, the impasse in the Constitutional Convention was resolved by a compromise stipulating that for representation and direct taxation a slave would count neither as a whole person nor as a non-person, but as three-fifths of a person. This was known as the "federal number," in which three-fifths of the slave population would be added to the entire white population for the purpose of determining the number of seats in the House of Representatives. The greater the number of seats in the House, the greater the direct taxation. This compromise gave the South 47 percent of the seats in the House, making it easier for the North to prevail on slavery issues. Because free blacks constituted 8 percent of the total population in 1790, as "free persons," they were, according to the clause, counted as full persons, like free whites, for purposes of representation. Both sides looked to the compromise's brighter side. According to Charles Pinckney, delegate of South Carolina, the southern delegates "made the best terms for the security of [slavery]. We would have made better if we could, but on the whole, I do not think them bad." At the same time, delegate James Wilson of Pennsylvania concluded that the northern delegates had succeeded in "laying the foundation for banishing slavery out of this country, albeit the period is more distant than I could wish. At the end, both the North and the South had compromised (174).

Colaiaco (2006) accepts that over the years, critics have alleged that the three-fifths clause reflects that the framers regarded slaves as less than complete humans. Modern neo-Garrisonian interpreters of the Constitution have condemned the framers, alleging that after proclaiming "all men are created equal" in the Declaration of Independence, they produced a Constitution that denied that blacks were men at all. However, the charge of relegating blacks to mere chattel status is more applicable to Justice Taney than to someone who understood the three-fifths clause as an unavoidable compromise. Regardless of whether sine framers believed that black persons were not entitled to full civic rights, the three-fifths clause had nothing to do with this prejudice. Northern delegates wanted to exclude blacks from being counted, not because they believed them to be less than human, but because they sought to weaken the power of the slaveholding South in Congress. At the same, southern delegates wanted every slave counted, not because they acknowledged that blacks were human beings equal to whites, but because they wanted to increase the voting power of the South in Congress. Colaiaco (2006) reveals that it became clear to Douglass that the three-fifths clause related not to the humanity or moral worth of slaves, but to their legal status. In fact, under the clause, free blacks would be counted as free persons for purposes of representation. The compromise was not about race, but about political and economic power. Douglass concluded that the three-fifths clause favored freedom by giving an increase of "two-fifths" of political power to free over slave states. He thus reinterpreted a clause usually condemned as favoring slavery into an outright disadvantage to the South. "Instead of encouraging slavery," Douglass concluded, the Constitution encourages freedom by holding out to every slaveholding State the inducement of an increase of two-fifths of political power by becoming a free State (p. 175).

Colaiaco (2006), wraps up his insightful study of Douglass, surprisingly with a chilling account of Lincoln's second inaugural address. The war that by now had claimed 620,000 Union and Confederate soldiers was still raging, a nightmare that Douglass had warned the country against from his early speeches in Rochester New York and other places around the country and around the world. Douglas had pressured his friend Lincoln to make the abolition of slavery the major war aim of the North, and to issue an Emancipation Proclamation that would end slavery once and for all, but it would take Lincoln another year before acceding to Douglass' request, dealing the death blow to slavery in the south and in the continental United States. In this inaugural address, Lincoln echoes Douglass' prophetic view of the Civil War before a throng of more than thirty thousand that had gathered in Washington to listen to the president's reflection on the carnage that had devastated the nation for four long years. As Lincoln stepped to the wooden platform erected for the event, standing before him amongst the crowd was Frederick Douglass, and standing on the balustrade above the president, was his future assassin, the actor John Wilkes Booth, a fervent supporter of slavery. Lincoln then admitted what Douglass had known from the beginning that slavery had been the cause of the war. Lincoln proclaimed that this terrible war was God's punishment against a sinful nation, adding that the South was punished for perpetuating slavery, and the North was punished for compromising with it. In addition, that slavery violated the Constitution ethical objectives to establish justice, secure the blessings of liberty, and promote the general welfare of all Americans. When Douglass was prevented from entering the reception that was held at the Executive Mansion that evening, Lincoln ordered that he be admitted, welcoming him warmly with the words: Here comes my friend Douglass. Affirming to Douglas that there is no man in the country whose opinion I value more than yours, he asked Douglass What he thought of the speech. Douglass responded: "Mr. Lincoln that was a sacred effort" (pp. 192, 193, 194). Colaiaco (2006) closes this section affirming that Frederick Douglas, the former slave, changed the course of American history, as he employed the full power of his oratory to unleash a storm of angry reproach against the institution of slavery. He was the nation's Gadfly, directing his wrath against the southern slaveholders who perpetuated the institution, against none-slaveholding southerners who supported the institution and against northerners who compromised with slavery. Douglass also directed his wrath against the hypocritical white church for justifying slavery and preaching submission. Exhibiting majesty in his eloquence Douglas insisted that until slavery was eradicated, America had no right to celebrate freedom, neither on the Fourth of July nor on any other day.

Woodson (1933) reveal that more than a century before Garvey's birth, Frederick Douglass was already embracing sound nationalist principles, arguing that it is vain to talk of being men if we fail to do the work of men. That we must endeavor to become uniquely valuable to society by building houses, rather than just living in them, by making shoes and clothes rather than just wearing them, and by planting and harvesting wheat and rye rather than just being consumers of these goods (p. 84). This was not a feature attributed to the constitutionalist and brilliant orator, but the revelation adds an extra quality to the brilliance we have come to know as Frederick Douglas.

While paling in comparison with the force of personality and accomplishment of Frederick Douglass the next two African American intellectuals are more easily recognized, these two are Booker T. Washington and W.E.B. Du Bois. Harlan (1983) relates a lifetime rivalry and cooperation between these two African American intellectual giants with a great deal of fairness, showing respect for both sides while inclining to neither. His book is about Du Bois but holding the mantle of leadership simultaneously made it inevitable for these two to have crossed each other's path continuously, as in the occasion when Du Bois and Washington ran into each other aboard an elevated train in New York. Washington was on his way to meet with Andrew Carnegie, and in making conversation, he asked Du Bois if he had read The Gospel of Wealth. Du Bois made it clear to him that he had not thought that book worth his time or interest. To which Washington replied, 'you should'. The statement may have left everyone else lost but Du Bois understood from it that Washington simply applied to Carnegie one of his own traits of character: that he had no faith in white people even though he was most popular among them. If he was talking with a white man he sat there and found out what the white man wanted him to say, and then as soon as possible he would say it. Harlan (1983) then commented that Du Bois was wrong about Washington's faith in white people, but he had insight into how Washington manipulated a cantankerous man of wealth such as Carnegie (p. 134). Here was Washington reaching out to a young man 12 years his junior and was rebuffed, but the seed of this rebuff was sewn much earlier. Du Bois (1903) reveals the story behind the disagreement between the two, as Du Bois characterized Washington as the leader of both races, as he sought to compromise between the South the North and the Negro. That this is an age when the more advanced races are coming in contact with the less developed ones, thereby intensifying the race feelings, and he saw it as unfortunate that at this very time, Washington would present a plan that in essence accepts the inferiority of Black People (p. 49).

In attempting to clarify the cause of this dispute Harlan (1983) commented that, "Du Bois' rejection of Washington was that his materialism and his compromise with white tyranny denied blacks their right to dream, to aspire and to master the world around them"(p. 51).

It is challenging scholars to understand why Du Bois could not just pursue his own goals of high intellectual development among those qualified Negroes, and allow others to develop along the line of industry and property ownership as Washington, and later Garvey proposed. Rather he spent a great deal of time and energy in berating the program of both these men, and particularly in the case of Marcus Garvey, who was a vicarious protégé of Washington, Du Bois lead to an anti-Garvey campaign that succeeded eventually in the deportation of this great leader back to his native Jamaica. Carlisle (1975) reminds us that although nationalism was important to all the leaders of the past, it was a viable and necessary alternative, given the desolation caused by the level of oppression. Washington and Du Bois were no exception to this, neither was

Douglas whose quote on nationalism is previously recorded in this book. There was one leader to whom nationalism
meant everything, and he staked his future on it. More than
any other leader of the twentieth century, Garvey brought
together separate streams of black nationalist thought, and
organized a mass movement around a coherent nationalist
ideology. If Garvey is not recognized for anything he
should at least be recognized for giving us a clear expression of Black Nationalist ideas and for leading a mass
movement equal to none (p. 121).

However, Marcus Garvey was heir to a rich tradition of
nationalistic ideas that had its genesis more than a century
before his birth. One example as Carlisle (1975) tells us, is
found in Paul Cuffe a free Negro who purchased, built and
captained ships that cross the Atlantic with passengers
seeking to  repatriate to their native Africa as early as
1811 (p.18). Other noted nationalists and emigrationists
were Paul Martin Delaney, Alexander Crummel and Edward Wilmot Blyden, their activities in the mid eighteen
hundreds ranged from lecturing to building organizations
capable of raising funds necessary for sailing ships across
the Atlantic for the purpose of repatriation (p. 80).

Another intellectual who wrote extensively on the subject "black slavery on subjugation" was the late Sir. Eric
Williams, former Prime Minister of the island of Trinidad.
Williams (1944) reminds us that initially, slavery was not
relegated to blacks; it was simply an issue of economics

spurred by the need for field hands in the tobacco, sugar and cocoa plantations. In the colonies and the Caribbean Islands the first workers were whites coming out of Great Britain as indentured servants. A racial twist was given to what was an economic phenomenon, and that out of this phenomenon a new one known as racism, was born. Un-free labor in the New World was brown, white, black and yellow; Catholic, Protestant and pagan. The first instance of slave trading in the New World involved the indigenous people of the area, but they rapidly succumbed to the ex-cessive labor demanded of them, the poor diet and the white man's discipline. These first indentured servants were poor whites, some came voluntarily and some were brought to the new world involuntarily. There was a posi-tive attraction from the new world and a natural repulsion from the old. In 1611 the governor of Virginia was willing to welcome convicts reprieved from death as a ready way to furnish the territory with men. But the labor of the in-dentured servants was not enough to supply the needs of the new territories, so they turned to Africa. (p. 6). Wil-liams (1944) is short on information as to how the Europe-ans were able to get to Africa, locate and dominate thou-sands of humans, pack them into the wholes of their ships and transport them back to the new world. Another Wil-liams, this one with the first name Chancellor, is more forthcoming in this regard. Williams (1987) tells us that at the beginning of the Atlantic slave trade in the sixteenth century many African chiefs and kings actually thought that the prisoners of war they were handing over to the Europeans were to be used as workers in some foreign endeavor. They profited handsomely from the exchange but supposedly they knew little of the ultimate aim, they also knew precious little of the ways of the Europeans they were now dealing with. They had no experience with the white man slave system or its equation with race. Even if this is offered as an excuse for the way things turned out ultimately, it underscores the fact that blacks must take responsibility for themselves and their future, after all the evidence reveal that they played a role in their own social and economic demise from the outset. Gunpowder and the weapon played a significant role in initiating and perpetuating the slave trade, a role perhaps as significant as that of religion and religious indoctrination.

The concluding thoughts on this chapter are that Mannings' analysis borders on the radical and there are few writers and intellectuals of any race who would dare take on the subject of religion with this much intensity. Manings is also removed from the non-religious writers and intellectuals who dedicate much of their time and energy gratuitously condemning religion as an all-around negative phenomenon. On the contrary he demonstrates intellectual maturity by giving the subject the respect it deserves if for no other reason than for the place it occupies in the hearts and minds of the believers realizing that persuasion through evidence is a more effective tool for the enlightening and liberation of those who experience the sense of imprisonment and oppression that invariably accompanies organized religion.

The African American family is a perfect example of a group that could use this persuasion as it navigates the murky waters of liberation employing the very tool that was used to enslave them several centuries earlier. The hope is that the presentation of these facts may be enough to have the members of the Black family overcome their fears of challenging the sacred tenets of a system that has overwhelming in their existence since their rapture from the African inlands.

Even though the expression black family may not have appeared too frequently in this report the implication is that when we speak of these intellectual giants who just happen to be black, and the highly productive activities they happened to have been involved in, alongside them there was a family, a nuclear or extended family that was also an integral part of these activities. These brilliant black men for the most part, had families of their own and these ideas and activities affected them significantly. The reaction of the sons and daughters of these great men and women who sought to lead the race in times of trouble is a story that is hardly ever told and one that this book seeks to draw attention to in its own way.

What I see to demonstrates is that not everyone was content with the status quo or with their position of second class citizenry, that throughout their captivity blacks have always sought to improve their lot and to defeat the stereotypes attached to them by other groups.

It should be clear by now that slavery would not have been possible without religious indoctrination, and in this case the religion in question is Christianity, the Euro-American version of that two thousand year old religion to which blacks have clung for their own salvation. Seeking to liberate themselves through the very religion responsible for their captivity and degradation is paradoxical at best, but the thought of not having a religion to turn to for refuge constantly proves to be too much for the vast majority of the ex-slaves.

The infantile notions of god and religion that the ex-slaves continue to cling to, appears to be the insurmountable barrier preventing blacks in the diaspora and on the continent from achieving the independence they've long sought.

# PSYCHOTHERAPY
# AND THE HEALING PROCESS

This book attempts to present a comprehensive review of the process we have come to know as psychotherapy, its history and the contribution it has made to overall human happiness and the advancement of the species. Dr. Jerome Frank's 1963 publication *Persuasion and Healing,* in which he compares the various therapeutic approaches of the past fifty years, will serve as a point of departure as I explore the multicultural dimension of the psychotherapeutic process, and the effectiveness of its application in a cross-cultural setting.

Some elements of advocacy will be added in the interest of change and improvement in the practice as we contemplate the swelling of the ranks of the emotionally disturbed and the mentally ill in the century that has elapsed since the process was first introduced.

Without pinpointing a particular time in history, it may be argued that the therapeutic process in its most rudimentary aspect had its beginning when the species developed the capabilities for reasoning and introspection. Reasoning and introspection therefore, it can be argued, are the foundations for philosophy, as humans began to ask questions regarding themselves and their environment, their origin, their destiny and the nature of God. Thinking through some of these and other questions, or as we call it; *philosophizing*; gave way to what then became religion. This deep thinking also gave way to the discipline we have come to know as psychology, a Greek term for the study of the soul. The Greeks equated the Psyche as the Soul, and

170

Logos in Greek symbolizes Study. A clear understanding of what we have come to know as the helping profession is important if we are to make these services available to a larger number of people in our society, recognize the generalized emotional malady that touches nearly everyone and eventually improve the efficacy of the healing that so many are so desperately in search of. Simplifying the process is crucial and by its very nature it is the most difficult part of the task for how one does make simple a process that is designed to treat those who are continuously in a crisis mode and convinced that their situation takes precedent over all else. Within the profession of psychology is where the study of human behavior became more focused, particularly as we strived to understand aberrant and unusual behavior, this perhaps is the greatest challenge faced by the profession then and now. For most of human history, people with strange and unusual behavior were treated by neurologists, physiologists, psychiatrists and other practitioners of the medical profession. It was not until 1874 when the German born Wilhelm Wundt (1832-1920), a physiologist himself wrote and published *Principles of Physiological Psychology,* (1904) that the idea of the psyche becoming a separate and distinct field of study began to take on an aura of reality.

Frank (1963), tell us that the range of people who receive psychotherapeutic services is very broad, ranging from those who simply need some help in having some of the burden of living lifted off their shoulders, to the severely ill with disturbances in thinking, feeling and behavior (p.8). Another way of putting it would be to say that the ultimate goal of psychotherapy is to assist the individual in knowing themselves more effectively, developing greater and more effective knowledge of the world and life, and effectively reconciling the two. If there is any element of truth in that statement, then we can safely conclude that psychotherapy, the process designed to improve the human psyche as well as the thinking process, is still in its infancy. This argument is made because even though most therapeutic interventions are aimed at assisting clients in the complex process of developing mechanisms, acceptance, fitting in, as well as countless other talking points, few if any of these therapeutic mechanisms offer the individual any more understanding of the physical world they live in, and their place in it. Most patients are being assisted in coping with a world they hardly understand, and in a large number of those cases the therapists are no better off when it comes to that particular subject.

The blurring of the line that separates facts from fiction creates a never ending and violent conflict inside the mind of many individuals, and this conflict leads to the type of confusion that effectively serves the interest of those with answers for which there are no evidences. These individuals, or groups as the case may be, use this confusion to their advantage promoting their brand of truth thus increasing the sense of guilt and confusion among the confused and most self harming behaviors are the result of confusion.

Psychologists and philosophers are yet to define ignorance and manipulation as the nemesis threatening sanity, security, world peace and individual happiness. Until they do, the revolving doors of therapeutic and behavioral centers everywhere may be swinging perpetually.

The misunderstanding of the lines of separation between psychiatry and psychology has not made this task any easier, for there are certain areas in which psychologist should not venture, and other areas in which the psychiatrist's presence often does more harm than good. Distinguishing the two and acting both forcefully and legally in the construct of that distinction is the psychologists' greatest challenge.

The psychiatrists, the medical doctor who specializes in the functioning or malfunctioning of the brain, assumes their superiority where matters of the psyche are concerned, hence, they do not perceive challenge of any kind, as far as the politics of this subject is concerned. They assume the psychologist's second tier status and often would venture to instruct him or her in the performance of their duties. However, understanding that some patients are in need of psychiatric care while others are in need of benign psychotherapeutic care, is crucial to this issue and its possible clarification.

But for a thorough understanding of the practice we have come to know as psychotherapy it is important to take a closer look at what we have come to know so far as human history, bearing in mind all of its contradictions and polemics surrounding the topic.

Homo sapiens is the term used to describe the creatures invested with the ability to reason, with the capacity for introspection and with the ability to resolve problems. To that, we may add language, although a voice box and vocal chords came some time after Homo sapiens developed basic problem solving skills.

With the rapid changes in technology and a transient society moving at speeds that very few are able to keep up with, there may never have been as great a demand for the therapeutic process and the sense of wellness it is expected to provide. Everyone from the high powered executive to the housewife, the lawyer, the builder, the doctor, and professions of all sorts, all are in need of the assertiveness and the coping mechanisms provided by those who are engaged in the helping profession.

Wherever two or more individuals get together with the distinct purpose of improving the emotional state or quality of thinking of the other or of each other, the therapeutic process is indeed manifesting itself. The level of training in this case is of secondary consequence; support groups and genuine friendship both meet this category as they play a role in the well-being of the individual. Undoubtedly, there are cases in which a more informed, well-trained professional may be needed to achieve for the individual, a level of clarity unavailable in those aforementioned circumstances, but proper support remains crucial particularly after the individual has had more in-depth professional psychotherapeutic intervention. This process is greatly aided when the professional makes it a point to be as inconspicuous as possible, informing and empowering the patient while at the same time reducing the possibility of dependency. Following statement from Marsha Linehan, inventor of Dialectical Behavior Therapy may go a long way in making that very point: "If they would act like themselves, they would [be better off]. . . All you are trying to be is simply one human being trying to help another human being. That's all this is." Unfortunately, the category mistake obscures that fact." The statement; which appeared in the March/ April edition of *Networker*; was made as part of her efforts to have her psychology students initiate their career with more effective methods in dealing with their clients and it In some ways the statement sums up feelings shared by some about psychotherapy, a practice that is unknown to many; and leaves confused others that have had exposure to its complex nature.

Much of the confusion surrounding psychotherapy may arise from the fact that it is a relatively new profession; one of the newest of the social sciences; and even though there have been newer practices since the emergence of psychotherapy, the excitement, drama, and controversy has brought it the continuous public attention. Psychology is still in the process of defining itself and fending off critics who still attempt to write the profession off as quackery or pseudoscience. However, for those who have assisted another human being in becoming even slightly more functional in a world overrun by madness, uncertainty and confusion, their feelings about this profession is an entirely different one.

These brave soldiers in the battle for clarity, understanding and self-realization for others, are the ultimate helpers, in need of no gratitude or rewards as they commit to their best efforts in improving the lives of those who seek them out for assistance. Their gratitude lies in the work they do, for it is highly gratifying, and their rewards; as the Christians would say; are in Heaven. Nevertheless, the one area in which psychotherapists owe themselves an extraordinary debt is in defining precisely the nature and purpose of their profession, this could be in part because of the blurring of the lines between psychiatry and psychology. There are certain areas in which psychologist should not venture, and other areas in which the psychiatrist's presence often does more harm than good. Distinguishing the two and acting both forcefully and legally in the construct of that distinction is the psychologist's greatest challenge.

The psychiatrists, the medical doctor who specializes in the functioning or malfunctioning of the brain, assumes their superiority where matters of the psyche are concerned hence, they do not perceive challenge of any kind, as far as the politics of this subject is concerned. They assume the psychologist's second tier status and often would venture to instruct him or her in the performance of their duties. But understanding that some patients are in need of psychiatric care while others are in need of benign psychotherapeutic care, is crucial to this issue and its possible clarification.

# THE HISTORY OF PSYCHOLOGY

For most of human history people with strange and unusual behavior were treated by neurologists, physiologists, psychiatrists and other practitioners of the medical profession. It was not until 1874 when the German born Wilhelm Wundt (1832-1920), a physiologist himself wrote and published *Principles of Physiological Psychology,* (1904) that the idea of the psyche becoming a separate and distinct field of study began to take on an aura of reality.    But Wundt never argued strongly for any particular theory. The theory closest associated with him was The Theory of Central Innervations, or the General Theory of the Molecular Processes in the Nerve-Cell. This theory was the result of a protracted research conducted on the nervous system prior to establishing his laboratory. The actual results of the research Rieber and Robinson (2001), tell us," cannot be summed up in a small space" (p. 51).  The research was highly complex, and loaded with scientific language related to neurological functioning.

Five years later in 1879, Wundt would establish one of the first formal laboratories for psychological research, at the University of Leipzig. With the creation of this laboratory, Wundt was able to explore the nature of religious beliefs, identify mental disorders and abnormal behavior, establishing psychology as an independent academic branch of study separate from all others.

Wundt's decision was considered a break with the past, a virtual shift in paradigm as it relates to the observance of aberrant behavior and the treatment of psychological disturbances, however, there were others thinking along similar lines,  because only a year later in 1880, the Viennese physician and psychiatrist Josef Breuer (1842-1925), was presented with a patient by the name of Bertha Pappenheim who suffered from paralysis in the extremities on the right side of her body, with hallucinations, frequent loss of consciousness, hearing impairments, speech impairments, and vision impairments.

Bertha's condition began to appear during the period in which she was helping to nurse her sick father. She told Breuer that she once woke up during the night in great anxiety about the patient, who was in a high fever; and she was under the strain of expecting the arrival of a surgeon from Vienna who was to00 operate. Her mother had gone away for a short time and Bertha was sitting at the bedside with her right arm over the back of her chair. She fell into a waking dream and saw a black snake coming towards the sick man from the wall to bite him.  She tried to keep the snake off, but it was as though she was paralyzed. Her right arm, over the back of the chair, had gone to sleep, and had become anesthetic and when she looked at it the fingers turned into little snakes with death's heads (the nails). Breuer suggested that it was probable that Bertha had tried to use her paralyzed right hand to drive off the snake and that its anesthesia and paralysis has consequently become  associated with the hallucination of the snake. When the snake vanished, in her terror she tried to pray. But language failed her: she could find no tongue  in which to speak, till at last she thought of some children's verses in English and then found herself able to think and pray in that language.

During this period Breuer was collaborating and conferring with Sigmund Freud, although there is no evidence that Freud himself met Bertha. In their conferences and correspondences the patient's name was concealed and a pseudonym was used to describe her instead of her birth name, in this case the name chosen was Fraulein Anna O. In describing Anna O to his colleagues Breuer (2004), stated that she was of considerable intelligence, remarkably acute powers of reasoning, and a clear sighted intuitive sense, he powerful mind could have digested, needed even, more substantial intellectual nourishment, but failed to receive it once she had left school. Breuer commented that her rich poetic and imaginative gifts were controlled by a very sharp and critical common sense a quality that also made her quite closed to suggestion. Only arguments had any influence on her, assertions were without effect. Her will was energetic tenacious and persistent.

Breuer (2004), tells us that one of Anna's principal traits was a sympathetic kindness. Even during her illness, she benefitted greatly from the care and support she gave to some sick and poor people. He described her as sexually undeveloped, as she reported to past or present amorous interest, and manifested no such thoughts even during her hallucinations.

Breuer diagnosed Anna O's illness as a case of hysteria and gradually developed a form of therapy which he believed was effective in relieving her symptoms. He came to the conclusion that when he could induce her to relate to him during the evening the content of her daytime hallucinations, she became calm and tranquil. Breuer himself saw this as a way of 'disposing' of the 'products' of Anna O.'s 'bad self' and understood it as a process of emotional catharsis. The patient herself described it as *chimney sweeping,* and as her own, *talking cure.*

Breuer informed us that at one point in her illness Anna O. declined to drink and would quench her thirst with fruit and melons. This condition lasted for several weeks until one evening, in a state of self-induced hypnosis, she described an occasion when she said she had been disgusted by the sight of a dog drinking out of a glass. Soon after this she asked for a drink and then woke from her hypnosis with a glass at her lips.

In his published account of the case, written some twelve years later, Breuer treated the story which Anna O. had related in a trance as a true account of an incident which had given rise to her aversion to drinking. He said he had concluded that the way to cure a particular symptom of 'hysteria' was to recreate the memory of the incident which had originally led to it and bring about emotional catharsis by inducing the patient to express any feeling associated with it.

The sudden disappearance of one of Anna O's many symptoms thus became the basis for what Breuer later described as a 'therapeutic technical procedure'. According to both Freud and Breuer, this method had been applied systematically to each of Anna's symptoms and as a result she was cured completely of her hysteria.

# THE CONTRIBUTION OF JEROME FRANK

In the introduction of Frank (1963) Norman Cousins states, "High on the list of medical achievements in the twentieth century is the increasing knowledge of the uniqueness of the human animal. This knowledge includes first of all, an understanding of the special qualities of the brain, not just as the seat of consciousness but as the control mechanism for bodily functions." (xi) The author of the book Jerome D. Frank, then proceeds to offer his own insight as it relates to the therapeutic process and those who take part in it. Frank tells us that "psychotherapy is commonly offered to those who seem basically intact yet are unable to handle environmental demands" (p.23).

Here again the distinction is drawn between patient and client, between the mentally ill, and the emotionally disturbed. Cousin's words remind us of the importance that lies in understanding that distinction. Cousins go on to note that,

> It is important for the individual to feel connected to the collective of the society itself, adding that, everyone has something important to contribute to the whole, and the radiating effects of that contribution are often beyond calculations. It is not enough to be told that we have powers far beyond our consciousness; the discovery of self and of the pathways to our potentialities is the most exciting adventure on earth (p. xii).

According to Cousins, all psychotherapy involves a setting and a conceptual framework that specifies the relationship between healer and patient. This involves the therapist's ability to inspire, clarify and facilitate. Cousins adds to this, the therapist's ability to alleviate patients sense of helplessness and powerlessness.

Frank (1961), makes reference to the various schools of psychotherapy and describes some of the basic components these schools are almost required to possess if they are to successfully provide services for those in need of it. With an adequate interpretation of Frank (1961) and other editions of this same writings these components may be narrowed down to six, and are applicable to any setting in which serious attempts are being made to improve the life and the thinking on those seeking services:

1.  The First of these of course is the trained socially sanctioned healer, whose healing powers are accepted by the sufferer and by his or her social group. This becomes the principal person designated to provide these services. One who is required to meet some intellectual standards, and certain standards of conduct as recognized by the community they belong to.
2.  The sufferer or patient is the focal point of the treatment, and he or she occupies the second place.
3.  The third of these components is the setting in which the healing, therapist or counseling is expected to take place.
4.  The fourth component is the setting in which the therapeutic relationship is expected to take place. This setting should be conducive to the patient or client achieving the level of comfort he or she requires in order to affect the necessary change. Serenity and neutrality are expected to be important components of this setting as

they allow for greater focus and attention on the part of the patient.

5. The fifth component is that the theory or method to be employed in improving the functionality of the patient/client must be clear enough to be understood by the patient. It should be in written form with verbal explanation following up for the purpose of clarifications.

6. Lastly, this theory must be practiced with integrity, following high ethical standards, and a high level of respect for the patient/client regardless of his or her socioeconomic background. All therapeutic, healing or counseling modalities should have these basic components if they are to be effective. It is nearly impossible to think of a treatment modality that does not comprise these modalities (pp. 2, 3.5).

Duncan, Miller and Sparks (2004), offer a similar suggestion as far as the necessary components for a treatment modality. They differ only in the sense that the client occupies the first place. This component is then followed by what is known as the therapeutic alliance they are convinced ought to exist between the patient and the therapist or healer. The third component in this modality is the model to be employed in achieving some improvement in the patients' functioning, and at the end they place the techniques that the modality utilizes for achieving its goals. Duncan et al (2004), add to these components an accurate analysis of the entire therapeutic structure including a criticism of the diagnosing procedure. They initiate this criticism by asking us to confront the unpleasant reality that the field of therapy is in trouble. They point to Schizophrenia, characterized by them as the King of Diagnosis, as the symbol for all that is wrong with psychotherapy, particularly its medical model. In their own words:

> Many, if not most, accept that schizophrenia is a lifelong struggle with mental illness only made somewhat manageable with medication—a catastrophic, if not hopeless, life of turmoil destitution, and despair. Many, if not most, have never heard of the Harding study (Harding, Zubin, & Strauss, 1987). Harding tracked down 269 clients who were admitted to Vermont hospitals with a diagnosis of schizophrenia—an average of thirty-two years after their first admission. She found that about two thirds of these former back ward patients showed no signs at all of schizophrenia and had long since stopped their medications! The "recovery" rate is astounding, considering the images that the label of schizophrenic typically brings to mind. Moreover, the clients reported the key to recovery had been finding a safe, decent place to live, and having a mentor, someone they trusted, who cared... Therapists—armed with the *DSM* required in their training, reinforced in licensure, and enforced by third-party payers—selectively listen to information that people present and focus on the very behaviors that confirm their expectations. Clients accept diagnosis as medical fact and become enslaved by its implications. As the extant literature proves, this process is robust, operates outside the range of awareness, and erodes the curative elements of therapy (pp. 27, 28).

Duncan et al (2004) then points to renowned psychiatrist Jerome Frank's 1973 observation that psychotherapy may be the only treatment that creates the illness it treats, and adds to that Kutchins and Kirk (1997) assessment of the economic side of Frank's observation arguing that the *DSM* transforms ordinary reactions to life stress into billable pathology, one in which everyone becomes a potential patient, and one in which diagnosis is altered capriciously to fit certain social patterns or norms. The most famous example of this they argue is homosexuality, which, unbelievably, was once regarded as a mental disorder. Homosexuality was "cured" by a vote of the American Psychiatric Association when gay activists protested being identified as sick. Duncan et al (2004) completes this criticism with a presentation of Kutchins and Kirk (1997) eye-opening account of the voting for and against different disorders on the part of the psychiatric profession, stating that it is based far more in politics and economics than on science, embracing their suggestion that the *DSM*'s language of mental illness is a self-serving political instrument rooted in psychiatrists' striving for credibility among their medical brethren.

The collusion between the drug companies and the medical professionals who strongly endorse the medical model for psychiatric treatment is one that Duncan et al (2004) is also very critical of. They introduce David Healy (1997) persuasive argument that in *The Antidepressant Era* drug companies are as much in the business of selling psychiatric diagnoses as they are of selling psychotropic drugs. The reason for this Healey (1997) argues is rather simple. One promotes the other, in doing so they capitalize on the public's propensity for believing medi-

185

cal authority. Healy (1997) then raises disturbing questions about how much the medical science of diagnosis is governed by financial interest. Most of the diagnosis, Duncan et al (2004) argues, fails to include contextual factors as it describes only individual behavior; it ignores relational, environmental, and cultural influences. Classifying only individual behavior as abnormal implies that when someone does not fit smoothly into his or her prescribed cultural role, it is that person who is at fault.

Duncan et al (2004) argue that the most insidious aspects of the diagnosis dilemma is that it often codifies racial and cultural prejudice and they point to recent studies with findings that both race and social status of children influenced the diagnoses and treatment they received.
Children who were culturally different than their helpers received more serious diagnoses and more drugs and were less likely to receive therapy (pp. 29, 30).

Jerome D. Frank may not have been a theorist but he offered some valuable insights and analysis regarding the therapeutic process, and in exploring the historical roots of psychotherapy, Frank (1961) reminds us that the efficacy of the psychotherapeutic method relies entirely on the participant's belief that the method actually works. Frank (1961), also alludes to of three basic and traditional methods of healing: the Religio-magical method, the Rhetorical method and finally the Empirical or Naturalistic method.

Franks speaks extensively of the Religio-magical method of healing, that is, the method in which a healer combines the roles of priests and physician, and refers to them as emotionally charged rites that require the participation of the sufferer and members of the family or social group. However, there is some lack of clarity in describing the other two forms of healings he mentioned, as he tells us is that Rhetorical healing implies symbolic and aesthetic experiences addressed only to the soul or spirit. On empirical healing all he tells us is that it combines physical and psychological methods.

We also understand from Frank (1963), that one of the principal objectives behind any therapeutic process is the enhancement of the patient's sense of mastery or self-efficacy, and he defines success in treatment as one that helps patients achieve an increase sense of inner freedom and satisfaction with their accomplishments. To be qualified as effective, all schools of psychotherapy are expected to bolster the patient's sense of mastery or self-efficacy in at least two ways: "by providing the patient with a conceptual scheme that explains symptoms and supplies the rationale and procedure for overcoming them, and second, by providing occasions for the patient to experience success" (pp. 48, 186). Frank (1963) then introduce us to the psychotherapeutic version of the Rumpelstilskin principle, thus named after the fairy tale in which the queen breaks the shrewd dwarf's powers over her by guessing his name. This principle in the therapeutic sense states that since words are a human being's chief tool for analyzing and organizing experiences, the conceptual scheme of all psychotherapies increase patients' sense of security and mastery by giving names to experiences that up until that point had appear confusing and inexplicable. Once the unconscious or ineffable has been put into words, it loses much of its power to terrify. This capacity to use verbal

187

reasoning to explore potential solutions to problems, Frank (1963) argues, also increases people's sense of their options and enhances their sense of control. It is not even required that the approach be correct in its theoretical framework, but rather that it be plausible (p. 48).

# THE BIRTH OF PSYCHOANALYSIS

In psychoanalysis too, the setting is crucial as comfort and relaxation is instrumental in getting the patient to verbalize all that concerns him or her and that could be the cause of the dys-functionality at that given moment in their lives. Trust in the practitioner is also of unique importance since it falls on them to interpret and makes some sense of all that the patient verbalizes.

The founder of this modality Sigmund Freud, never actually met Bertha Pappenheim or Anna O, but her story, as related to him through Joseph Breuer fascinated him and served as the basis for *Studies on Hysteria* (1895), a book co-written by Breuer and Freud. Breuer's description of her treatment led Freud to conclude that hysteria was rooted in childhood sexual abuse.

Freud's insistence on sexuality as a cause eventually led to a rift with Breuer, who did not share this view on the origination of hysteria. "The plunging into sexuality in theory and practice is not to my taste," Breuer explained (Grubin, 2002). While the friendship and collaboration soon ended, Freud would continue his work in the development of talk therapy as a treatment for mental illness.

The case of Anna O. played a fundamental role in the devel-opment of Freud's thought. She has frequently been described as the first psychoanalytic patient, a view which Freud himself, lecturing at Clark University in the United States, once en-dorsed.

Her statement that being able to verbalize her problem helped her to unburden herself is in accordance with the treatment later denoted in psychoanalysis as the catharsis theory. Accordingly, Freud described her as the actual founder of the psychoanalytic approach.

Free Association also came into being after Anna decided (with Breuer's input) to end her hypnosis sessions and merely talk to Breuer, saying anything that came into her mind. She called this method of communication "chimney sweeping", and this served as the beginning of free association.

Anna's case also shed light for the first time on the phenomenon called transference, where the patient's feelings toward a significant figure in his/her life are redirected onto the therapist. By transference, Anna imagined to be pregnant with the doctor's baby. She experienced nausea and all the pregnancy symptoms. After this incident, Breuer stopped treating her.

In her introduction Breuer (2004), Rachel Bowlby reiterated that, "It was Anna O herself who, famously, named this the talking cure, surely the mother of all sound bites, and as telling a catch phrase for what was not yet psychoanalysis as anyone could have dreamt up. It happens that the phrase talking cure was first uttered in English, although Anna O's first language was German"(p. x). Breuer tells us that the English phrase was uttered in a moment when Anna O was compulsively speaking in languages other than German. She would speak in Italian, French and particularly in English.

# DUNCAN MILLER AND SPARKS

In *The Heroic Client,* Duncan, Miller and Sparks (2004), makes a similar criticism of what is now version IV of the DSM, or DSM IV and its usefulness, or lack thereof, in diagnosing and treating of the mentally ill. Duncan et, al use one of Sigmund Freud's famous quotes to illustrate their opinion of the manual. The quote in question, "I have found little that is good about human beings, in my experience, most of them are trash" (p. 23). Duncan et al, singles out Borderline personality disorder as an example of what Freud would consider to be trash for reasons that are hard to understand. The reason behind this may be the difficulty that lies in treating BPD clients that come into treatment, since they are rated as being unstable in mood, self-image and relationships. Their emotions are also said to be erratic, and to vary capriciously from day to day. Borderline patients are further described as manipulative, argumentative, irritable, clueless regarding their identity, and uncertain regarding their values, loyalties and choices (p. 46). What Duncan et al (2004), is conveying is that borderline personality is the ultimate test for any therapist. They are no doubt the patients most in need of treatment, yet they are the patients most therapists seek to avoid. They require of the therapist, an inordinate capacity for patience, tolerance, equanimity and poise, features most therapist are not endowed with. They are the neediest patients and the ones facing the greatest danger, so the question to be raised is; were they born that way or were these conditions acquired? It is here that the opening statement of book is worth repeating, "If they would act like themselves, they would [be

better off]. . . . All you are trying to be is simply one human being trying to help another human being. That's all this is."

Duncan et al (2004), delivers a scathing indictment of psychotherapeutic treatment and the direction in which it is head-
ing. Most of their focus is on psychiatry or the medical aspect
of treatment. They tells us: "With the smog certainty of a book-
ie, the prosecuting doctor serves as judge and jury" (p. 214).
For those limited in eloquence those few words sum up much of
their feelings in connection with the health care system, more
specifically the mental health system. It is obvious that the classification and stigmatizing of patients is of great concern to
them, and it is almost certain that their campaign, as manifested
through their writings, will land on deaf ears.

Duncan et, al (2004), are strong promoters of the therapeutic
process, one in which respect for and participation of clients is
encouraged, but they also recognize that psychotherapy cannot
begin to compete with the billion dollar drug industry when it
comes to promoting the value of the therapy even though the
data is clear that psychotherapy is as good if not better than
medication when the two are compared.

Duncan et al (2004), criticism is not just limited to the medical or psychiatric field, they also rail against the system that
idolizes, and mythologizes therapists as healers thus marginaliz-
ing the client and preventing him or her from participating in
their own positive change. In satire and sarcasm they note," The
therapist's understanding of the intricacies of the human psyche,
the complexities of emotional experience, and the secret dynam-
ics of human relationships enable clients to change. The light of
the therapist's wisdom is a beacon that shines the way to peace,

happiness, and self-actualization (p.55). It is hard to imagine such eloquence expressed in mockery or satire but that is precisely how this statement was utilized. The fact is that there are times and places in which this image of the therapist is indeed helpful, where this image is indeed a positive one.

The dodo bird verdict is another concept to which Duncan et al (2004), introduce us. This concept relates to the various theories in the field of psychotherapy competing for supremacy. This dodo verdict is borrowed from the *Alice in Wonderland* fable in which everyone is declared a winner and should all be given prizes. This analogy is used by Duncan et al (2004), to illustrate the fact that there is no one-treatment method that stands above the others. Duncan et al (2004), reminds us that there has been an unprecedented expansion in the number of mental health practitioners, and that the abundance of therapists would inevitably fuel a competition between psychologist and psychiatrists, as well as a competition for clients between the two groups.

Another idea that Duncan et al (2004), rails against is the idea of therapist presenting themselves as individuals with a respectable body of knowledge in order to provide adequate care and guidance to those who seek their assistance. The concept of a special protocol for each form of ailment is also met with scorn and ridicule by them. It is almost as if in their minds, clients are a monolith, that the word client references a particular group or class of people. My own experience has taught me that not all clients wish to actively participate in structuring their own treatment. Some have a need to trust and be led by someone who has demonstrated an adequate capacity to guide and care for them, and this is especially so when the expressed goal of the process is to empower the client, setting him or her on a path to freedom, from their own fears, their own misconceptions, and their own confusions.

In their book *Narrative Means to Therapeutic End,* White & Epston deal extensively with the subject of empowerment, and treat it as a concept that is intrinsically bound with knowledge. The French intellectual Michael Fucault is introduced as a means of strengthening and illustrating their argument. We find therefore in White & Epston (1990), "In considering the constitutive dimension of power, Fucault concludes that power and knowledge are inseparable—so much so that he prefers to place the terms together as power/knowledge or knowledge/power" (p.21). The competing ideas of power, truth, knowledge and social control that frequently make their way into psychotherapy, are discussed using Fucault's ideas of knowledge and power but we are still left wanting for clarity, for the subject is far from being simple.

White & Epston's efforts appears to be aimed at explaining and even re-defining the therapeutic process, even questioning at one point the validity of the term: "We believe that therapy as a term is inadequate to describe the work discussed here. The Penguin Macquarie Dictionary describes therapy as a treatment of disease, defect etc., as by some remedial or curative process" (p.14). The exact point White & Epston are attempting to convey with this remark is not exactly clear, but it highlights the ongoing efforts of those in the field of psychology and psychotherapy to re-define its meaning and to consolidate it as a profession. It may be worth closing this short revue of White & Epston (1990), with the following:

> In striving to make sense of life, persons face the task of arranging their experiences of events in sequences across time in such a way as to arrive at a coherent account of themselves and the world around them. Specific experiences of the past and present, and those that are predicted to occur in the future, must be connected in a lineal sequence to develop this account. This account can be referred to as a story of self-narrative (p. 10).

Two other major treatment modalities have emerged since the days of Freud and Breuer. Rational Emotive Behavior Therapy, created around the middle of the twentieth century, and Motivational Enhancement Therapy or MET, a more recently created treatment modality.

Rational Emotive Behavior Therapy was introduced to the world in 1955 by Albert Ellis (1913-2007) an American psychologist who held M.A. and Ph.D. degrees in clinical psychology from Columbia University.

In defining the nature of psychological disturbance and health Ellis and Dryden (1997) argue that the biological tendency of humans to think irrationally and dysfunctionally has a notable impact on such disturbance:

> At the heart of neurotic disturbance lies the tendency of humans to make devout, absolutist evaluations of the perceived events in their lives. As has been shown, these evaluations are couched in the form of dogmatic must's, should's, have to's, got to's, and ought's. We hypothesize that these absolutistic cognitions are at the core of a

philosophy of devout Beliefs that is a central feature of much human emotional and behavioral disturbances. Tese Beliefs are deemed to be irrational in REBT theory in that they usually (but not invariably) impede and obstruct people in the pursuit of their basic goals and purposes (p.14).

Ellis and Dryden (1997) note that the "role of Rational Emotive Behavioral Therapists is to unconditionally accept their clients as fallible human beings who often act self-defeatingly but are never essentially bad (or good) " (p. 27). Ellis and Dryden (1997) added that, " REBT practitioners pay particular attention to other ways that humans perpetuate their psychological problems and attempt to asses these carefully in therap. Therapist are often aware that much dysfunctional behavior is defensive and help their clients to identify the irrational Beliefs that underlie such defensive dysfunctional behavior" (42).

Rational Emotive Therapy, called Rational Emotional Behavior Therapy since 1993 (REBT), argues that all people are born with self-defeating tendencies. When something goes against their goals, values or desires, usually things such as failure, rejection, etc., they have a choice of feeling healthier emotions such as feeling sorrow, disappointment, and frustration, which encourages them to go back and change the adversities they face. Or, humans have a choice of making themselves terrified, panicked, depressed, self-pitying, self-doubting, etc.

Ellis and Dryden (1997) commented that emotions people choose mainly depend on their belief systems. It is not so much a question of their goals and values but what they tell themselves when those goals and values are thwarted or blocked.

And they have a rational set of beliefs or what we call 'preferences,' rational, meaning self-helping beliefs, such as "I don't like what is going on; I wish it weren't so, how annoying;' let's see what I can do about it." Or, humans very frequently pick irrational beliefs or what we call 'demands,' such as "because I don't like what is going on, it absolutely should not exist, it must not be, I can't stand it, it's horrible, I think I'll kill myself etc." There are only three basic demands that lead to most of what we call neurotic behavior. One is, "I must do well and be loved by people or I am no good" which leads to depression, terror, self-doubting, feelings of inadequacy, etc. Two, "You people absolutely must treat me kindly, nobly, and considerately, or you are worthless, you are no good," and that create anger, rage, wars, genocide, etc. And three, "conditions under which I live in the environment must absolutely be better than they are, they must give me exactly what I want, and never really deprive me," and then it is "horrible, terrible, and awful" when conditions are not the way they must be (p. 45, 46, 142, 144).

Ellis and Dryden (1997) argue that REBT is more philosophical than the other therapies because you change your basic outlook, and give up those musts, shoulds, oughts, and demands and just go back to having preferences. "I would like to do well but I never have to; it would be great if you treat me kindly but you obviously don't have to" and if you do, then you would rarely make yourself neurotic. And if people use a whole variety of cognitive, emotive, and behavioral techniques which REBT shows them how to use, then by working very hard against their upbringing and their biology, they could make themselves significantly less disturbed (p. 4, 91, 145).

It is hard to speak of Albert Ellis without at some point mentioning Aaron Beck. They are contemporaries, and from the reading there does appear to have been an element of symbiosis between the two, but it is easy to see which is more dominant between the two. In the Albert Ellis reader, which he co-wrote with Shawn Blau 1998, Ellis offers a partial autobiography, written in very crude and colorful language, with four letter words and all. It is one of the few writings in which he refers to his friend and colleague Aaron Beck. In it he referenced a conference held on the Evolution of Psychotherapy, one that is held every five years lead by the Milton Erickson foundation. Outstanding therapists like Victor Frankl, Carl Rogers and Rollo May were present. In relating the event, Ellis quoted his friend Aaron Beck's who made a comment regarding his performance:

> There is no question that [Ellis] was the pioneer in modern day psychotherapy. He really cleared the road for the rest of us who followed behind him….He is absolutely right about the should and the musts…I do want to…personally thank him for what he has done in helping me to develop my own therapeutic techniques" (p. 330).

In return Ellis thanked Tim Beck for doing so much research to promote and develop Cognitive Therapy, a concept for which Beck is widely credited in the therapeutic community.

The final therapeutic concept to be discussed in this research is that of Motivational Enhancement Therapy. This treatment approach was elaborated by psychologists William R Miller,

<u>Ph.D.</u> and <u>Stephen Rollnick</u>, <u>Ph.D.</u> and documented in their 1978 publication entitled *Motivational Interviewing*. The therapy itself is a more in-depth, hands-on application of the theory described in Motivational Interviewing, and it is described as a systematic intervention approach for evoking change based on the principles of motivational psychology. The method is client centered, and it is designed to produce rapid, internally-motivated change in behavior primarily in problem drinkers, but it has proven effective in curbing the behavior of other chemical dependent clients.

We learn from Miller and Rollnick (1987), that at the heart of Motivational Enhancement Therapy lies in Carl Rogers articulated and tested theory about critical skills on the part of the counselors, for facilitating change, adding that the counselor's role is not a directive one in providing solutions, suggestions, or analysis. Instead, the counselor need only offer these three critical conditions to prepare the way for natural change: accurate empathy, non-possessive warmth, and genuineness (p.6).

# MESMER AND HYPNOTHERAPY

Hypnotherapy is perhaps the intervention that best illustrates the second component in the list of four as described earlier, that is the component related to the proper setting. If we understand nothing else of hypnotherapy we do at least understand that a serene and peaceful setting is required if the patient is to succeed at focusing on the hypnotist words and achieve the goals he or she is seeking to obtain through the help of the hypnotist. Frank (1963) credits Franz Anton Mesmer with the emergence of hypnotherapy as a distinct form of healing; this is because of Mesmer's ability to relieve patients of their symptoms by putting them into a trance, adding that Mesmerism was the form of healing that preceded psychotherapy. Frank (1963), tells us very emphatically that all human behavior reflects the need to make sense of the world, and he adds that a major function of theology is to assign a divine purpose to all that happens, especially those that appear random or unjust and adds that these psychotic delusions reflect patient's desperate efforts to make sense out of their inexplicable experiences.

The second chapter of the book, the writer tells us, is dedicated to outlining the rhetorical framework for psychotherapy, and in it Frank (1963), offers some clear and constructive criticism of psychology and psychotherapy. Frank (1963) begins with an unequivocal criticism of the plethora of psychotherapeutic approaches with this comment: "In our present state of ignorance the most reasonable assumption, already mentioned, is that all enduring forms of psychotherapy must do some good or they would disappear"(p. 19). The quote highlights the fact that there is great similarity across the board in the success rate of the various therapeutic modalities, perhaps underscoring the notion that the functioning word is care, and that it is the concept of care that patient or client respond to more so than the particular technique that is applied to their condition. This of course does not apply to those patients with more severe mental illness; it is a foregone conclusion that these require more in-depth treatment, in a residential setting and often requiring medication.

In a rather disconcerting and nearly bewildering statement Frank (1963) tells us: "The psychiatric patient, the ill savage, the person on the verge of religious conversion, and the prisoner of the communists all are in distress because of their inability to master certain stresses, which arise in large part from their interactions with other persons or groups, present or past" (p. 19). This last quote from Jerome Frank is not easily discernible, and requires further analysis. The intent of the analysis is easily understood, but the choice of words is no,t. When is it acceptable to refer to our fellow humans as *ill savages,* and how does the person on the verge of a religious conversion or the prisoner of communists fit in all of this?

Frank (1963), notes that therapeutic methods can be loosely classified in two basic groups: directive and evocative. As the name describes it, directive therapy is one in which the clinician asserts him or herself in guiding the patient's actions towards the changes needed to resolve the problems that brought them into treatment. They are characterized by efforts on the part of the therapist to correct the patient's symptoms or maladaptive behavior through advice and persuasion (p.145, 146). In a later version of the same book, there is a variation in the description of direct individual psychotherapy. We find in Frank & Frank (1991) "The effects of such social variables as ethnicity, economic status, and education on the diagnosis and treatment of mental illness provides further evidence that these are culturally biased enterprises" (p. 10). Hollingshed & Redlick (1959), is invoked to inform us that, "lower-class minority patients were likely to receive directive treatment, often accompanied by medication. Patients who were better off or more educated, by contrast, were more likely to receive permissive forms of treatment stressing insight" (p.10). The example of directive individual psychotherapy Frank (1961), uses to illustrate this point is at best unsettling. We find in this example something that borders on a cure of homosexuality. Not only that, the example is prefaced with the following caveat: "Many patients with sexual deviations do not respond to this or any other form of psychotherapy" (p. 149). The example used is hat of a thirty five year old man whose sexual contacts up until that point were that of the same sex. He suffered periodic attacks of chess pain and palpitation, and was overly dependent on his parents. The patient however, had abandoned his teaching career to take over his father's business after the latter had suffered a stroke. Since the patient had come to the therapist for some understanding of his homosexual behavior, that issue was dealt with head on, but more from the point of assisting the patient in overcoming his fear of rejection, especially from girls. In a few weeks, this fear was overcome and the other health symptoms had also disappeared, and in twelve weeks the patient was involved in a healthy heterosexual relationship. Frank (1961, and Frank &

Frank 1991), refer to this as a successful treatment of subjective symptoms and behavioral difficulty by "rational psychotherapy," and added that the unusually favorable outcome should not be regarded as typical (p. 149). The illustration is well understood, but one has to wonder if it was necessary to preamble it with the statement of deviant behavior. The last place same sex individuals expect to hear words that invokes prejudice is from therapist or psychiatrists documenting their findings.

Evocative forms of therapy on the other hand, are more in tuned with Sigmund Freud form of psychoanalysis, despite the fact that in our times, so many have turned away from that approach. It is designed to assist the patient to achieve insight into his or her feelings and behavior, and stress his or her ability to express this insight in words. This approach demands on the patient, greater maturity, spontaneity and a higher degree of freedom than in directive therapy. The major difference between these two therefore, is that directive therapy tends to be circumscribed, while the evocative technique tends to be more open-ended. Thusly, it tends to appeal to the more educated members of our society, those who place a significantly higher value on self-knowledge and on verbal skills. Frank (1963), notes that, in an attempt to prevent the patient from developing an unrealistic dependence and to strengthen his autonomy, the therapist in this approach, attempts to follow the patient's lead, and to talk about what is on the patient's mind, openly admitting or pretending to be ignorant and unable to comprehend (p. 153).

Frank (1963) states convincingly that all forms of psychotherapy are valid else they would cease to exist a claim that should not go unchallenged since we have seen a variety of bad practices in many fields of endeavor that have actually remained in business for a long time. Psychotherapy is no exception in that respect, for if a patient comes into treatment with a delusion that he or she is involved in a special relationship with God, and that special relationship places him or her above others in terms of intrinsic worth, it may be irresponsible on the part of the therapist not to attempt to bring that client/patient closer to the reality regarding themselves, their world and that of the rest of his fellow humans. The DSM IV (1995), describes this condition as a form of delusional disorder of the grandiose type whose symptom are that of inflated worth, power, and knowledge with special relationship to a deity or famous person (p. 154). Patients coming in to treatment with such misconception and suffering the damage of their own delusional behavior, are done no good service, when we respect these views and send them back out to the world with just better coping skills. Unless the foundations of their irrationality is shaken severely, it may be difficult for such patients to make any improvement in behavior. The treatment modality that succeeds at connecting well with the client/patient may be said to be effective, but if it fails at connecting the patient/client with his or her reality then its validity may come into question.

Frank (1963), deals extensively with the concept of self-healing attributing it in part to the patient's expectations of help. This of course applies entirely to the religio-magical form of healing since the healing that takes place within the psychotherapeutic process is of a different type. Healing in this case refers to the process in which the patient/client is no longer haunted by the pain of the traumatic experience and is able to function within the society with diminished pain, diminished anger and diminished self-destructive behavior.

Frank & Frank (1961, 1973, 1991), also weighs in on the criticism of the diagnosis debate and the current state of pharmacotherapy by arguing that the DSM is a classification scheme that has had an enormous and justified impact on every aspect of psychiatric research and practice except psychotherapy, and that this is because the phenomenological classification of disorder made by the manual is only able to work with that which could be measured. In following this reasoning, the experts who put together the manual often ignore the meaning patients ascribe to their symptoms, as well as the social and historical antecedents of the patient's suffering when putting together their diagnosis. But free from the constraints of the diagnosis, psychotherapy is able to effective address those concerns of the patient (p. 10).

# OTHER THINKERS AND THEORISTS

There are those who argue that Psychoanalysis was born not, as is frequently claimed, out of the foibles of emotionally unstable middle-class women who came to consult Freud in Vienna. It was born amidst the florid and sometimes extreme physical symptoms displayed by patients who had been consigned to one of France's greatest hospitals – La Salpêtrière in Paris. The original begetter of the theory of unconscious symptom-formation – a theory which lies at the heart of psychoanalysis – was not Freud, nor even Breuer, but Jean Martin Charcot.

Charcot was not a psychologist, he was a neurologist. His greatest gift was a genius for anatomical dissection and post-mortem diagnosis. His greatest handicap was that he practiced neurology at a time when techniques of tissue-staining were primitive, X rays had not been discovered and the instruments of investigation which have made modern neuroscience possible did not exist. The electroencephalogram (EEG), which would revolutionize neurology and psychiatry, was not in general use until the 1940s. Other techniques for brain-imaging, such as Magnetic Resonance Imaging (MRI), were not introduced until the closing decades of the twentieth century. Even today, at the beginning of the twenty-first century, the process of charting the brain's intricate functioning has barely begun. As Rita Carter (1999), writes in her book *Mapping the Mind*, "the vision of the brain we have now is probably no more complete or accurate than a sixteenth-century map of the world" (p. 8).

A writer and medical journalist, Rita Carter takes a gratui-tous swipe at Freud when she argues that there is an almost complete lack of evidence of the efficacy Freudian psychoanalysis as a therapy. Carter came to that remark after some analysis of the process of rationalization that people engage in to justify their behavior or the choices they make. She states that, "you do not have to use much imagination to realize how much a process might be used to dignify emotional or arbitrary acts in ordinary life: choosing to employ a person of one color, for example, over that of another"(p. 42). Suddenly, the issue of race is introduced, swiftly and directly, as images of prejudice and discrimination are instantly conjured up.

Traditionally, race has not played much of a role in psychoanalysis, particularly since its pioneers, both in Europe and America avoided the subject. Referring to this very subject Houghton Brodrick (1960) commented: "The fact is that the word race should be left to the racist and not used in speaking or writing about anthropological matters. There is only on race of men, and that is the human race" (p.31). Not only does academe avoid the issue, it also fails to shed light on the more enlightened side of the conversation as Houghton Brodrick suggested, and in avoiding the subject of race academe has deprived itself of a point, a passion and an energy that may well be useful in the resolution of many other issues. This is because the men and women in academia that are of direct African ancestry rarely develop their fullest intellectual potentials while avoiding that issue. When the issue of race is brought up it creates discomfort so they avoid it, and again, in avoiding this most pertinent issue, their contribution is only a fraction of what it could be. Carter equates Freudian psychoanalysis with continuous rationalization, thus omitting or dismissing the idea of the catharsis, and the many benefits this process has delivered over the years.

The efficacy of talk therapy and the entire psychoanalytical movement that followed, came into question almost at its inception, for there are those who continue to argue that Bertha Pappenheim did not improve under Breuer's care and that her cure did not come about until after her subsequent hospitalizations. For this reason, it is important to revisit Breuer's first observations when meeting Bertha that she had a keen intellect, a craving for psychic fodder, which she did not receive after she left school. In addition, that she was endowed with a sensitivity for poetry and fantasy, which was however, controlled by a very strong and critical mind. Apparently, these are the qualities Bertha took into her post treatment life as a Jewish activist and intellectual. Loentz (2007), reports that:

> Pappenheim became the founder of the League of Jewish Women (*Jüdischer Frauenbund, JFB*) and was elected its first president. She remained president of the organization for twenty years and served on its executive board until 1934. The JFB joined the Federation of German Women's Association, becoming its largest organizational member; and Pepperheim was a member of the executive board of the *BDF* for ten years (1914-1924). Although its platform and projects changed over time, reflecting Germany's changing political and social climate and economic conditions, the *JFB* remained steadfastly committed to the goals of the *moderate* German women's movement, tailoring these to the specific

concerns of Jewish women and the Jewish community as a whole (p.50).

This aspect of Anna O's life is hardly ever revealed, and this holds true for the rest of the psychotherapeutic movement, as a story whose full scope is still being revealed.

# THE HEALING PROCESS

Having glanced over some of the more popular treatment methodologies over the past century, the focus of this second half of the book is on the healing process, and for that we return to Jerome Frank. Two types of healing will be discussed in this section, one is the spontaneous religio-magical form of healing highlighted in Frank (1963), and the other is the process through which victims of abuse reduce the pain anger and confusion they carry as part of their daily lives. The latter is often a result of the patient having found a therapeutic intervention that functions for them, thus allowing them to put their lives and everything around them in a more functional perspective.

Frank (1963), is not too clear on the concept of religio-magical healing, as he combines it with empirical healing, naturalistic healing, and rhetorical healing, all in a structure that makes it difficult to tell one from the other (p. 3). Frank (1963), argues that psychoanalytically and existentially based therapies have much in common; the philosophy of existence shared by existential therapy brings their work closer to the religio-magical and rhetorical forms of healing primarily because of their stress on immediate experience (p.6). We know from evidence that there has been over the millenniums, a variety of processes that claim to have had healing capacities for those who believe in them. Shamans, high priest, preachers and witch doctors of all sorts, have operated in all cultures taking credit for the remission of ailments on the part of their adherents, but as to be expected, their claims have been questionable. This forces us to deal with the question of "cure", a word that is banded around a great deal since the times of the shamans and witch doctors, but has also endured to become part of the lexicon of many therapists and therapeutic communities. The danger behind this habit is that relapse and recidivism has its way of making cure a relative term, for the question that must be asked is, how long does the remission or recovery have to last for it to be considered a cure? If the psychotic episode, the hallucination or the schizophrenic manifestation re-occurs after some time, can it really be referred to as a cure. Perhaps this is why in Frank (1963) we find the admission that psychotherapy itself cannot cure most psychoses; raising the question if it can actually cure any psychoses. Frank (1963) admits however, that psychotherapy does play its part in the management of psychological conditions (p. 11). What we do find in Frank (1963) however, is a rather eloquent definition for psychotherapy, describing it as the form of therapy in which the healing powers of the individual sufferer are brought out through psychological means. The behavior of humans towards each other in the environment is also made a part of the healing process, as this relationship with others shape attitudes, and worldviews and ultimately our sense of well-being (p.1). How and why these ancient methods work, and the precise reason why some of these modern techniques are effective still escapes us, according to Frank (1963), and that appears to be the major unanswered question they all possess in common, for an approach that works for one individual with the same illness, may have negative consequences for another. It is this conundrum that Frank (1963) attempts to guide us through as he analyses the complexities of the interaction of mind and body, and how belief systems affects the healing process.

We may well conclude based on Frank (1963), that healing is perpetual, that it is constantly taking place as long as humans are interacting with each other in a multitude of circumstances, it is a generalized but fair conclusion given all that has been said on the issue.

On the subject of traditional religio-magical healing Frank (1963) remarked that healing ceremonies are dramatic and emotionally charged rituals performed in an atmosphere of shared ideologies, one in which the subject's expectations of cure are heightened thus facilitating cure or at least its appearance (p. 65, 105, 108, 191).  But in many cases these expectations are also heightened in modern psychotherapy, at least during its early days. Frank (1993) makes reference to Franz Anton Mesmer whose dramatic performances marked the beginning of psychotherapy as a distinct form of healing as Mesmer was able to make his subject's symptoms go away by putting them in a trance. Healing through talk then followed, as demonstrated through Freud and Breuer, and it continues to be the most popular form of therapy in our times as it incorporates Frank (1963) definition of psychotherapy as a process designed to bring out the cure that lies within the individual (p.1).

To conclude this chapter it may be said that too few of the theorists include in their protocol or strategy an address of the major maltreatment each generation of humans continue to mete out to minors. To concur with the rest of the society that the treatment is not as bad as in the remote past when infanticide was common, cannot be accepted when the origin is psychotherapy. Children maltreatment in the form of rape and violent physical abuse is given little attention in therapy, and the few adults who survive the horror are often told to forgive and to move on, while the same treatment is being meted out to a new generation of vulnerable human beings. The therapeutic profession has done magnificently well in avoiding this issue, for reasons that are hard to understand. Granted, the pain and suffering generated in the clinician who has assist the human being in working through his or her trauma; regardless of their level of training; may be overwhelming and often too much for a great many, but it is here that the profession is called on to prove itself. According to deMause (1974), Freud himself did not believe the stories of children being abused by their parents and others, Freud referred to most of them as originating from childhood fantasy (p. 49). If Freud is admittedly the father of psychotherapy, then it is fair to conclude that this profession had a built in denial since its inception, at least as far as the issue of child abuse is concerned. To add insult to injury, before the profession considers the magnitude and importance of this issue, it has already turned to group therapy as a pre-eminent form of treatment, to the detriment of private interventions, the ideal setting for uncovering these long held painful secrets. Such private painful matters simply cannot be revealed in a group setting, it would be clearly irresponsible. The attempts to write these situations off as Post Traumatic Stress Disorder, is also troubling to these survivors.

All the fancy and elaborate psychotherapeutic models conjured up to date have done little to soothe the pain and anguish of those children who were ravaged, and nothing prevents them from living those horrors on a daily basis. All the fancy and elaborate psychotherapeutic models have done little to empower those children, to assist them in getting to a point where the savagery they endured no longer cause them to self destroy. That recurring aspect of human behavior is both denied and ignored until one of us, any of us, is confronted with the barrel of a gun, with one of the survivors whose anger and hate inches him closer and closer to pulling the trigger.

It is rather unfortunate that students are not allowed to express their opinions when it comes to research papers, even at a graduate level, but there is a new dimension in human behavior that psychology has been unwilling to address. This dimension is the level of anger and the wholesale gratuitous slaughter that anger is now responsible for. It is manifesting itself in the inner cities of the United States and in many developing countries, and its underreporting may be attributed to the fact that it is not yet penetrated the inner sanctums of the developed societies. It has remained so far a story of mutual destruction on the part of others. The expectations are that at some point, the field of psychology will venture into a thorough and in-depth analysis of this troubling phenomenon and its origins. Ours is a troubled society in desperate need of healing, but the healing begins with the individual, and not until a proper mechanism for healing is in place, will society itself be healed.

Finally, it can be said that this paper has become more than just an act of fulfilling an academic requirement, it is in reality a blueprint for making of psychotherapy a more effective process serving a larger number of people, particularly those who had neither herd of the term and those who have never really benefitted by its practice. It is a blueprint for a new and deeper approach to psychotherapy, one that will assist patient/clients in placing myth and superstition in their proper perspective thus allowing patient/clients to relate more effectively with their reality.

# A TREATISE ON HEALTH

I would be remiss if I should complete this literary work without some focus on a subject that is vitally important to all; the subject of health. When speaking of health a few terms stand out; terms the reader must be familiar with. These terms are, among other: Nutrition, Infection, Inflammation, Oxidation, Antioxidants, Free Radicals, Bacteria, Anti-bacteria, Viruses, Anti-virals.

## Nutrition

The process by which a living organism assimilates food and uses it for growth and for replacement of tissues. It is interesting that the French do not have a word for food, that in reality their term for food is really Nourriture or Nutriment. It is also interesting that the French are slim and trim for the most part. On the other hand, Americans and those cultures that imitate their diet of fast food and foods high in carbohydrates are mostly overweight if not obese. The lack of emphasis on nutrition has taken its toll on the health of far too many in the United States and around the world.

## Infection

An Infection is the invasion of any host organism by another living body in this case a virus or a bacteria. One of the main differences between these two is size, bacteria can be seen looked at under a microscope, but because of their diminutive size, viruses avoid detection even under the best microscopes. That is why combating viral infection is challenging to scientists. The most famous of all viruses known to humans is the Human Immunodeficiency Virus or HIV. The presence of this virus in the human organism is only detected when T helper cells within the host body are called upon to defend against the invader.

## Inflammation

The defense system within the host's body comes alive or ignites as it goes into action against the invading virus or bacteria, causing what is referred to, as an Inflammation. Some of the classical by-products of this inflammation are redness, heat, swelling and pain as the body initiates a desperate attempt to heal itself.

## Oxidation

Oxidation is a reaction in which the atoms in an element lose electrons and the valence of the element is correspondingly increased. We have all become familiar with the term antioxidant, what it means, and the role this term plays in preventing diseases. However, before we can speak of antioxidants, it is imperative that we at least attempt to describe the oxidation process that occurs within the cells of living organisms. The unfortunate thing here is that the description of oxidation is highly complex in nature, and requires an advanced understanding of chemistry.

By now there should be fair understanding that living organisms, humans included; are made up of cells, and that all cells possess a nucleus. The nucleus is the heart and soul of the cell, and two elements make up its essence:

Protons, which are positively charged, and electrons, which are negatively charged. The electrical charges in this case are irrelevant but worth mentioning at least for future conversations. But to return to this challenging description of oxidation it must first be said that in addition to the cells that make up the human body, each cells is made up of different types of molecules, and each of these molecules consist of one or more atoms of one or more elements joined by chemical bonds. The number of protons (positively charged particles) in the atoms nucleus determines the number of electrons (negtive ly charged particles) surrounding the atom. Electrons are involved in chemical reactions and are the substance that bonds atoms together to form molecules. Electrons surround, or "orbit" an atom in one or more shells. The innermost shell is full when it has two electrons. When the first shell is full, electrons begin to fill the second shell. When the second shell has eight electrons, it is full, and so on. The most important structural feature of an atom for determining its chemical behavior is the number of

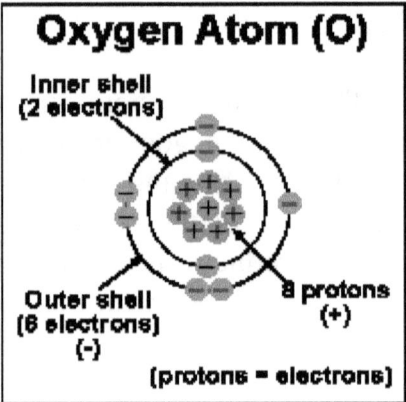

**Oxygen Atom (O)**

Inner shell
(2 electrons)

Outer shell
(8 electrons)
(-)

8 protons
(+)

(protons = electrons)

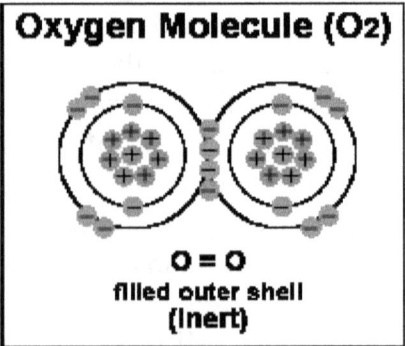

**Oxygen Molecule (O2)**

O = O
filled outer shell
(inert)

electrons in its outer shell. A substance that has a full outer shell tends not to enter in chemical reactions (an inert substance). Because atoms seek to reach a state of maximum stability, an atom will try to fill its outer shell by:

- Gaining or losing electrons to either fill or empty its outer shell
- Sharing its electrons by bonding together with other atoms in order to complete its outer shell

Atoms often complete their outer shells by sharing electrons with other atoms. By sharing electrons, the atoms are bound together and satisfy the conditions of maximum stability for the molecule.

## The Formation of Free Radicals

Normally, bonds do not split in a way that leaves a molecule with an odd, unpaired electron. However, when weak bonds split, free radicals are formed. Free radicals are very unstable and react quickly with other compounds, trying to capture the needed electron to gain stability. Generally, free radicals attack the nearest stable molecule, "stealing" its electron. When the "attacked" molecule loses its electron, it becomes a free radical itself, beginning a chain reaction. Once the process is started, it can cascade, finally resulting in the disruption of a living cell. Some free radicals arise normally during metabolism. Sometimes the body's immune system's cells purposefully create them to neutralize viruses and bacteria. However, environmental factors such as pollution, radiation, cigarette smoke and herbicides can also spawn free radicals. Normally, the body can handle free radicals, but if antioxidants are unavailable, or if the free-radical production becomes excessive, damage can occur. Of particular importance is that free radical damage accumulates with age.

## Bacteria

Bacteria is considered any numerous groups of microscopic one-celled organisms constituting the phylum Schizomycota, of the kingdom Monera, various species of which are involved in infectious diseases, nitrogen fixation, fermentation, or putrefaction. An anti-bacterial agent could be a synthetic or natural compound, which inhibits the growth and division of bacteria

## Viruses

Viruses are parasites with a non-cellular structure composed mainly of nucleic acid within a protein coat. Most viruses are too small to be seen with the light microscope and therefore must be studied by electron microscopes. In one stage of their life cycle, in which they are free and infectious, virus particles do not carry out the functions of living cells, such as respiration and growth. In the other stage, however, viruses enter living plants, animals or bacterial cells and make use of the host cell's chemical energy and its protein and nucleic acid synthesizing ability to replicate themselves. An anti-viral destroys viruses or suppresses their replication, or an agent that so acts.

# FOODS HIGH IN ANTIOXIDANT

Interestingly enough many of the foods we consume are high in antioxidants, these foods include dry beans, berries of various types including coffee, walnut, pecans, and most dietary vegetables. The vitamins C and E are thought to protect the body against the destructive effects of free radicals. Foods that are considered high in Vitamin C are Berries, Broccoli, Brussels sprouts, cantaloupe, cauliflower, grapefruit, honeydew, kale, kiwi, mangoes, nectarines, orange, papaya, red, green, or yellow peppers, snow peas, sweet potato, strawberries, and tomatoes. Foods with a high content of vitamin E are Broccoli, carrots, chard, mustard and turnip greens, mangoes, nuts, papaya, pumpkin, red peppers, spinach, and sunflower seeds. Antioxidants neutralize free radicals by donating one of their own electrons, ending the electron-"stealing" reaction. The antioxidant nutrients themselves do not become free radicals by donating an electron because they are stable in either form. They act as scavengers, helping to prevent cell and tissue damage that could lead to cellular damage and disease. According to research Vitamin E is by far the most abundant fat-soluble antioxidant in the body, and one of the most efficient chain-breaking antioxidants available. It is a primary defender against oxidation, and a primary defender against lipid peroxidation (creation of unstable molecules containing more oxygen than is usual). Vitamin C on the other hand is the most abundant water-soluble antioxidant in the body and it acts primarily in cellular fluid, it is particularly helpful in combating free-radical formation caused by pollution and cigarette smoke, and it plays a role returning vitamin E to its active form. Studies show that each of these vitamins has its own particular role in preventing some forms of cancer. Vitamin E is said to protect against cardiovascular disease by defending against LDL oxidation and artery-clogging plaque formation, and high dosage of vitamin C has been proven effective against all forms of cancer. The following are foods high in antioxidants that the reader may chose to focus on in order to assist in improving their overall health. Apricots, asparagus, beets, broccoli, cantaloupe, carrots, corn, green peppers, kale, mangoes, turnip and collard greens, nectarines, peaches, pink grapefruit, pumpkin, squash, spinach, sweet potato, tangerines, tomatoes, and watermelon, prunes, apples, raisins, plums, red grapes, alfalfa sprouts, green onions, onions, and eggplant. The Zinc and Selenium found in Red Meat, Sea Food and Poultry are also a good source of antioxidants.

## BANTING THE FIRST MODERN DIET

Charlotte Edwards reveals how a short, fat Victorian funeral director became a household name with a dietary regime amazingly similar to the most current food fad. On the August morning that he began his diet, 26 years into the reign of Queen Victoria, the short and very fat William Banting heaved himself out of bed at 8am, hoisted a corset around his bulging stomach and struggled into his three-piece suit. Unable to reach his laces, he gingerly eased his feet into his shoes with a boot hook - taking care as he stooped not to stress the angry boils on his buttocks. As he negotiated the stairs in reverse (a method, he found, that eased the crushing pressure on his knees), he was looking forward to the cooked breakfast awaiting in the dining room below - but dreading the effect it would have on his ever-ballooning bulk. Twelve months later, the 5ft 5in Mr. Banting, had shed more than three stone to be a slightly portly 11 stone. It was 1863 and Banting declared the diet "simply miraculous". So evangelical was Banting in extolling and promoting the virtues of his diet that he became a household name: the verb, to bant, meaning to diet, was absorbed into the vernacular and appeared in the Oxford dictionary until 1963. But in the century between Banting first taking a knife and fork to his new diet revolution and his last appearance in the OED, his name gradually slipped from the public consciousness . . . until, in 1972, an Amer-

ican cardiologist by the name of Dr. Robert Atkins published his own New Diet Revolution. Today, the Atkins
diet is the household name and Banting is forgotten by all
except a few students of dietetic history and a handful of
lexicographers. Yet, remarkably, the Atkins diet is virtually identical to that which stripped William Banting of his
excess pounds. So who was this low-carb, high-protein pi-
oneer for what is now a multi-million pound industry that
numbers among its devotees such Hollywood stars as Jen-
nifer Aniston, Demi Moore and Renee Zellweger? And
how did he discover his diet? William Banting, born in
London in 1797, was an upper middle class funeral director, and for five generations the family firm held the Royal
warrant until 1928. Among those whose state burials they
organized, were Admiral Nelson, George III, George IV,
William IV and Prince Albert (just two years before William began his diet). Later, under the reigns of his second
son, the company oversaw the funeral of Queen Victoria in
1901. The Banting family business paid for his Georgian
townhouse in Kensington, which was lavishly decorated
and furnished. His wife, Mary Ann, had a jewelry collec-
tion worth several thousands of pounds and, in the base-
ment of their four-story property, he kept an enviable wine
cellar which he passed on to his eight children (two boys,
six girls) in his will which would be worth £3.3 million today. From his mid-30s he struggled miserably against his
burgeoning size. None of his family suffered from obesity,

a condition, he viewed with "inexpressible dread". He blamed it for the catalogue of ills he suffered over the next 30 years: failing sight, impaired hearing, insomnia, an umbilical rupture, "many obnoxious boils, and two rather formidable carbuncles". He was so stung by the sniggers and snide asides of strangers as he waddled to his office at 27 St James's Street off Piccadilly, that he avoided social gatherings and public transport to escape, "the sneers and remarks of the cruel and injudicious".  Like his counterparts today, Banting tried every fashionable remedy on offer. In addition to regular trips to "the waters and climate of Leamington", Cheltenham and Harrogate, popular Victorian spa towns, Banting took up to three Turkish baths a week and only lost six pounds. He even experimented with starvation diets, living "upon sixpence a day, so to speak".. Yet "the evil", as he describes his fat, "still increased". A doctor and personal friend recommended extreme physical exertion: brisk walks, horse-riding and rowing on the Thames early every morning. "It is true I gained muscular vigour," Banting admitted, "but with it a prodigious appetite, which I was compelled to indulge, and consequently increased in weight, until my kind old friend advised me to forsake the exercise." Banting arrived at the Soho Square practice of Dr William Harvey, a distinguished surgeon, by chance. His usual specialist had taken his annual summer holiday, so Banting sought an alternative. Dr. Harvey was available and, again by chance, had just returned from a

225

Paris conference where he had heard a Monsieur Claude Bernard lecture on diet and diabetes. It occurred to Harvey that Banting would be the perfect candidate for M. Bernard's ideas for reducing excess weight in any individual male of or female. Harvey took copious notes as Banting described his daily dietary intake: the breakfasts that included umpteen slices of buttered toast and a pint of tea with plenty of sugar; much bread and other forms of carbohydrate. For lunch Banting was used to eating meat, pastry, more bread and beer, followed by sweet tea; and a supper of bread, milk and a fruit tart.

After taking copious notes, Dr. Harvey ordered Banting to cut out potatoes, bread, sugar, milk and beer. He handed him a sheet of paper which detailed his new regimen: "Breakfast, 9am: 6oz of either beef, mutton, kidneys, broiled fish, bacon or cold meat of any kind except pork or veal; 9oz of tea or coffee without milk or sugar; a little biscuit or 1oz of dry toast. "Lunch, 2pm: 5-6 oz of any fish except salmon, herrings or eels, or any meat except pork or veal; any vegetable except potato, parsnip or beetroot, turnip or carrot; 1oz of dry toast; fruit out of a pudding, not sweetened; any kind of poultry or game; 2-3 glasses of good claret, sherry or Madeira. Champagne, port and beer were forbidden.

"Tea, 6pm: 2-3oz of cooked fruit, a rusk or two, tea without milk or sugar."Supper, 9pm: 3-4oz of meat or fish similar to lunch. For nightcap, if required, a tumbler of grog (gin, whisky or brandy, without sugar) or a glass or two of claret or sherry."

Banting was so delighted with the prescription that he tipped Dr. Harvey £50 to give to his favorite hospital, on top of the usual fee. He wrote: "It certainly appears to me that my present dietary table is far superior to the former [and] more luxurious and liberal." It also worked. From the first week the undertaker began to shed pounds and as the months passed and his weight loss continued, Banting decided to share his "philosopher's stone" with the public. "Of all the parasites that affect humanity, I do not know of . . . any more distressing than that of obesity," he began his Letter on Corpulence in 1864. "I am desirous of circulating my humble knowledge and experience for the benefit of other sufferers, with an earnest hope that it may lead to the same comfort and happiness I now feel under the extraordinary change." While Dr. Atkins, who died earlier this year, reaped millions from his diet, Banting asked for no recompense for his publications. Indeed, he saw it as a public duty to pass on the "cure" for obesity and gave all the profits from the many editions of Letter on Corpulence to hospital charities. The Letter sold 63,000 copies in Britain - a staggering number in an era when many were illiterate - was translated into French and German, and sold widely in Europe and the US. Banting's once portly form was regularly satirised in Punch cartoons, even long after his death; his name was used in music hall ballads and the diet was even referred to by Evelyn Waugh in A Handful of Dust. Neither Banting nor Harvey made any attempt to copyright the idea, believing that the outline of the diet was "as old as the hills". Banting's descendants and biographers are scathing of Dr. Atkins's "reinvention" of the low-carb diet. Dr. Barry Groves, a nutritionist and author of Eat Fat Get Thin, says: "There is only one difference between the two diets: the quantity of carbohydrate allowed in Atkins is marginally less than in Banting's. I believe the extent that carbohydrate is restricted in Atkins is what makes it dangerous. Banting's diet was in fact more healthy." Banting's papers - his letters, diary, details of where he was educated - were inherited by his great granddaughter-in-law, Nina Banting, who destroyed them in a bout of post-natal depression in the late 1950s, describing him as a "horrid little man." Nina's grandson, the Rev David Banting, from Harold Wood, Essex, says: "I believe my ancestor was a philanthropist and the fact that he did not attempt to profit from the diet is typical of the public-spirited Victorian age. He had a good heart and, in a time when dieting was not that common, he wanted to share with others in his position, his great find. He wanted the world to know."

Like its modern day reincarnation, however, Banting's diet also caused controversy. In a time when Mrs. Isabella Beeton's newly published recipe book - filled with stodgy puddings and pies - was considered a domestic bible, a backlash was inevitable. Some newspapers reported gleefully that Banting had been killed by his own diet, a slight that he quickly rebuked in person. (Atkins, who died earlier this year after slipping on an icy pavement, was also incorrectly reported to have died from a heart attack brought on by his own diet.)   Banting was most frustrated by his lack of graphic evidence of the efficacy of his diet plan; something he believed would have silenced his critics and encouraged his adherents. "I deeply regret not having secured a photographic portrait of my original figure in 1862, to place in juxtaposition with one of my present form," he wrote. "It might have amused some, but certainly would have been very convincing to others and astonishing to all." Instead, he was forced to illustrate the change in the only way available, "putting on my former clothing, over what I now wear, which is a thoroughly convincing proof of the remarkable change." While no photograph of that survives either, it may have consoled Banting to know that, 140 years on, his diet really is world renowned, albeit under another name.

## TRANS FATS

Many of the random compounds created when oils are hydrogenated are so-called "trans-fats" or, more correctly, trans-fatty acids. These are unnatural compounds, which are known to be detrimental to health. In order to understand why, we need to consider some of the chemistry involved. (not too much, I promise). A natural, unsaturated fatty acid might look like the molecule below. It has several double-bonds between adjacent carbon atoms, which is what makes it "unsaturated". (saturated fats have no double bonds and all the "spaces" available are taken up by hydrogen atoms.

(These diagrams are simplified for easier understanding)

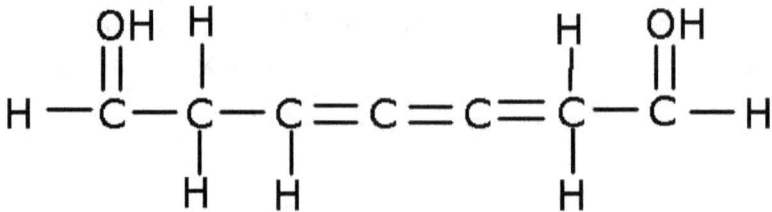

### Polyunsaturated fatty acid

When this oil is hydrogenated, it is not possible to control where the hydrogen atoms are added to the structure. If both hydrogen atoms are added to the same side of the structure, it is called a "Cis" fat. Cis fats exist naturally and, because the hydrogen atoms are crowded on one side of the molecule, they bend, allowing other chemicals and enzymes to bind to them.

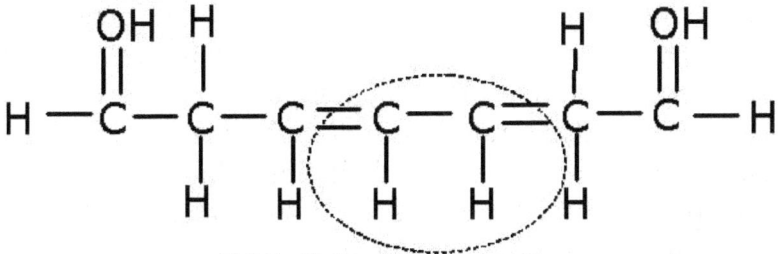

"Cis" fatty acid

If, however one hydrogen atom adds to one side of the structure and the other atom to the other side, it creates trans-fats, like the one below. Trans fats do not exist naturally, with a very few exceptions. Because the structure is un-crowded, they do not bend and so other molecules and enzymes find it more difficult to bind to them. The shape of the molecule is therefore vital to its function, much in the same way as the shape of a key is important for the operation of a lock.

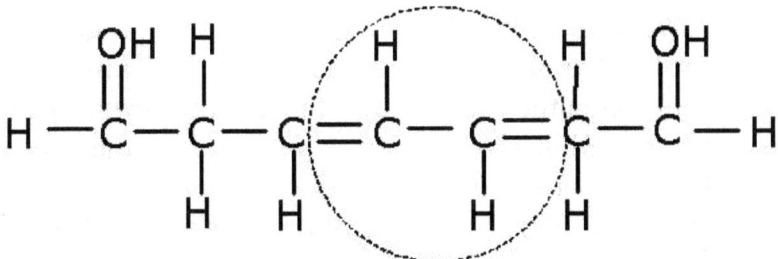

"Trans" fatty acid

In fact, it is the very fact that they are straight that allows trans-fats to solidify at room temperature. Natural, cis fats are curved and so cannot pack into a crystal formation at normal temperatures. Trans-fats, on the other hand, are straight and CAN pack into a crystal formation, which allows them to solidify at room temperature. As early as 1958 Dr. Ancel Keys reported that he believed that hydrogenated vegetable oils with their trans-fats components were responsible for the sudden and significant increase in ischemic heart disease over the previous decade. The response was predictable - the oil manufacturers buried the research and began the false attack on animal fats. More recently in 1978 University of Maryland researcher Dr. Mary Enig proved that the increased cancer rates were directly associated with total fat intake and vegetable fat intake, but not with consumption of animal fat. Dr. Enig, who is a consultant clinician, specializing in nutrition has since spent the last 25 years warning of the dangers of trans-fats and the relative safety of animal fats. It is said also that the Harvard School of Public Health has issued a warning regarding the consumption of margarines, snack foods and other foods containing hydrogenated oils (and their trans-fats), in favor of butter. More recently, concern over the role of trans-fats in disease has led a number of major food companies to remove these components from their products. This is probably a response to the recent FDA ruling that, as of 2006, all food labels must include the proportion of trans-fats in addition to other fat content. For now, a good guide is the amount of hydrogenated fat, and how high up the list of ingredients it is. The higher the listing, the more trans-fat there is. If you want to be more specific, add up the listings of the other fats and take it away from the total fat content, the difference is usually all trans-fats. If this is too much, there are a few simple rules you can use to avoid trans-fats. Firstly, avoid all products that list hydrogenated oil as an ingredient. Secondly, use only natural vegetable oil or animal-based fats (butter, ghee, lard, dripping) for cooking. If there is not a nutritional label on the food you buy, the recommendation is to avoid it since it cannot be determined if trans-fat is part of its makeup. See below some foods that often contain trans-fats and that should be avoided among others:

Micro-wave popcorn, potato chips, margarine, shortening, cake mixes and frostings, pancake and waffle mixes, certain ice-creams, non-dairy creamers, certain frozen dinners, and packaged puddings, . It is recommendable to read the labels of every food before purchase.

# *Bibliography*

Appleby Joyce, Hunt, Lynn. Jacob, Margaret.
   *Telling the Truth About History* W. W. Norton &
   Company, Inc. New York 1994.

Ardrey, Robert. (1963). *African Genesis: A Personal
   Investigation into the Animal Origins and Nature of
   Man.* New York N.Y. Delta Books.

Aries, Phillip. (1960). *Centuries of Childhood: A Social
   History of Family Life.* New York, N.Y. Vintage
   Books.

Barrow, R. & Woods, G. (2006). *An introduction to
   philosophy of education.* New York N.Y
   Routledge.

Barrow, R. Bailey, R. Carr, D., & McCarthy, C. (2010).
   *The SAGE handbook of philosophy of education.*
   Thousand Oaks CA. Sage Publication.

Benoit Denizet-Lewis Times Mag June 25, 2006
      Horacio Salinas

Bethesda Md. National Institute on Alcohol Addiction

Blau, T. H. (1988). *Psychotherapy tradecraft: the tech
   nique and style of doing therapy,* Bristol Pa. The
   Taylor Francis Group.

Borden, W. (1999). *Comparative approaches in brief dy
   namic psychotherapy.* Binghamton N.Y. Haworth
   Press.

Bradley, K., & Cartledge, P. (2011). *The Cambridge world history of slavery: Volume 1.* New York NY: Cambridge University Press.

Breuer, J. Freud, S, and Luckhurst, N. (2004). *Studies in Hysteria.* New York. Penguin Books.

Bringuier, J.C., & Piaget, J. (1977). Conversations with Jean Piaget. France Editions Laffont, S.A

**Brodie**, F. (1971). *No man knows my history: The life of Joseph Smith, the Mormon prophet.* New York N.Y. Alfred A. Knopf Publishers.

Bushman, R., & Woodworth, J. (2005). *Joseph Smith: Rough stone rolling.* New York N.Y. Alfred A. Knopf Publishers.

Carlisle, R. (1975). *The Roots of black nationalism.* Port Washington NY: National University Press.

Carter, R. (1999). *Mapping the Mind.* Berkeley and Los Angeles. University of California Press

Colaiaco, J. (2006). *Frederick Douglass and the Fourth of July.* New York NY: Palgrave Macmillan.

deMause, Lloyd. (1974). *The History of Childhood.* New York, N.Y. The Psychohistory Press.

deMause, Lloyd. (1992). *The History of Child Abuse.* The Journal of Psychohistory, 25. (3).

de Mause, Lloyd. (2002). *The Emotional Life of Nations.* New York. Other Press LLC.

Despert, L. (1970). *The Emotionally Disturbed Child:*

*An Inquiry Into Family Patterns.* Garden City N.Y. Double Day & Company, Inc.

Dewey, J.(1900). *The School and Society.* Chicago Ill. The University of Chicago Press.

Dewey, J. (1902). *The School and Society.* Chicago IL The University of Chicago Press.

Dewey, J. (1922). *Democracy and Education: An intro* Point Books

Dodds, A. (2009). *The Abrahamic faiths? Continuity and discontinuity in Christian and   Islamic doctrine.* Evangelical Quarterly, 81   (3), pp 24, 230, 253.

Douglas, F. (1852). *Fourth of July Speech.* [Online] www.freemaninstitute.org

Du Bois, W. E. B. (1903). *The souls of black folks.* Chicago IL: A.C. McClurg & Co.

Duncan, B.  Miller, S,  and Sparks, J. (2004). *The Heroic Client, A Revolutionary Way to Improve Effectiveness Through  Client-Directed, Outcome-Informed Therapy.*San Francisco, CA.  Jossey-Bass, Publishers.

Ellis, A.  (No date). *The Essence of Rational Emotive Behavioral Therapy.* Available (Online): http://www.rebt.ws/albertellisbiography.html

Ellis, A. &  Dryden, W. (1997).*The Practice of Rational Emotive Behavior Therapy.* New York Springer Publishing Company.

Ellis, A. & Blau, S. (1998). *The Albert Ellis reader: a guide to well-being using rational emotive behavior therapy.*  New York.  Kensington Publishing Corporation.

Ellis, A. (2002). *Overcoming Resistance.* New York N.Y. Springer Publishing Company.

Erikson, E. (1980). Identity and the life cycle, Volume 1. New York W.W. Norton & Company, Inc.

Frank, J.D. & Frank, B. (1961,1973, 1991). *Persuasion & Healing.* The John Hopkins University Press

Frankl, V. (1992). *Man's search for meaning: an introduc tion to logo-therapy.* Boston MA. Beacon Press.

Gates, H. L. (1994). *Frederick Douglass autobiographies.* New York NY: Literary Classics of The United States.

Genovese, E.(1972). *Roll jordan roll, The world the slaves made.* New York, NY: Random House Inc.

Green, D. (). *Hidden lives: voices of children in Latin America and the Caribbean.* London. Cassell Wellington House.

Harlan, L. (1983). *Booker T. Washington: The wizard of Tuskegee.* New York. NY: Oxford University Press

Harris, S. (2005). *The end of faith: religion, terror, and the future of reason.* New York N.Y. W. W. Norton & Company.

Harrison, V.(2006). *Scientific and religious worldviews: antagonism, non-antagonistic incommensurability and complementarity.* Heythrop Journal, 47 (3). P. 18, 349-366.

Haugen, Brenda (2006). *Joseph Stalin: Dictator of the Soviet Union.* Minneapolis MN. Compass Point

Books.

Ikeda, D. (2001). *Soka Education: A Buddhist Vision for teachers, Students and Parents* Santa Monica, CA.

Jessop, F. &, <u>Brown</u>, P. (2010). *Church of lies.* San Francisco CA. Jossey-Bass.

*Journal of the American Medical Association.* December 25, 2002 288,. 24, pp. 3096-3101Middleway Press.

Kramer, R. (1976). *Maria Montessori: a biography.* Chicago Ill. University of Chicago Press.

Levering, D. (2000). *W.E.B Du Bois—the fight for equality and the American century, 1919-1963.* New York, NY: Henry Holt and Company, LLC.

Lloyd, P. & Fernyhough, C.(1999). *Lev Vygotsky: critical assessments, Volume 1.* New York Rutledge.

Loentz, Elizabeth. (2007). *Let me continue to speak the truth:Bertha Pappenheim as author and activist.* Jerusalem Hebrew Union College Press.

MacMillan, Margaret. *Dangerous Games, The Uses and Abuses of History.* The Modern Library Books, a Division of Random House New York, 2008.

Manning, S. (2004). *Psychology, symbolism, and the sacred: Confronting religious dysfunction in a changing world.* **Otsego MI: Page Free Publishing, Inc**

<u>McGinn, L.</u> (1997). <u>American Journal of Psychotherapy.</u> 51 (3),pp 309, 8

Miller, A.(1998). *The Political Consequences of Child Abuse.* The Journal of Psychohistory, 26. (2).

Miller, A., & Jenkins, A. (2010). *Free from lies: Discover ing your true needs.* New York NY: W.W. Norton and Company Inc.

Miller, W. R. & Rollnick, S. (1987). *Motivational inter viewing: preparing people for change.*

Miller, W. R. (1994). *Motivational enhancement therapy manual: a clinical research guide for therapists treating individuals with alcohol abuse and depend- ency Volume 20*

Montessori, M. & Wyman, H.(1912). *The Montessori Method:Scientific pedagogy as applied to children in education.* New York Frederick A. Stokes company

Montessori, M.(2004). The Discovery of the Child. Delhi India. Aakar Books.

Mooney, C.G.(2000). *Theories of Childhood. An Introduc- tion to Dewey, Montessori*

Moore, J. (1965). *Booker T. Washington, W.E.B. Du Bois, and the struggle for racial uplift.* Wilmington, DE. Scholarly Resources Inc.

Payne, G. H., & Jacobi, A. (1916). *The Child in Human Progress.* New York. G. P. Putnam's Sons.

Poussant, A. (2000). *Lay My Burden Down: Suicide and the Mental Health Crisis Among AfricanAmericans.* Boston MA. Beacon Press.

Press.Woodson, C.G. (1933). *The mis-education of the Ne- gro.* Washington, DC: The Associate Publishers Inc.

Reuter, C. (2004). My life is a weapon: The history of sui- cide bombing. Princeton N.J Princeton University Press.

Riak, J. (2009). *Plain Talk About Spanking.* Available
    [Online] http://www.nospank.net/pt2009.htm
Rieber, R. and Robinson, D. (2001). *Wilhelm Wundt
    In history: the making of a scientific psychology.*
    New York Plenum Publishers.
Robinson, B.A. Jul 25, 2004 *Ontario consultants on Reli-
    gious Tolerance* Retrieved 1/11/11
    http://www.religioustolerance.org/flds.htm
Roekeach, M. (1960). *Understanding human values: Indi-
    vidual and societal.* New York, NY: The Free Press.
Scott, E. & Stowe, L. (1910). *Booker T. Washington,
    builder of a civilization.* Cambridge, MA: Andover-
    Harvard Theological Library.
Spindel, Donna J. *Assessing Memory,* Twentieth Century
    Slave Narratives Reconsidered Journal of Interdis-
    ciplinary History, Vol. 27. No. 2 (Autumn, 1996).
    Pp.247-261. Published by: MIT Press
Straus, Murray A. Donnelly, Denise. *Beating the devil out
    of them: corporal punishment in  American families
    and its effects on children.*  New Brunswick.
    Transaction Publishers.
Strauss, Murray. (2009). University of New Hampshire
    *Children Who Are Spanked Have Lower IQs*, New
    Research Finds. *Science Daily.* Available (Online)
    http://www.sciencedaily.com
United Nations *Declaration of the Rights of the Child.*
    Availble[Online]www2.ohchr.org/English/law/crc.htm.

Verhellen, E. (1996).*Monitoring Children's Rights.* The Hague, the Netherlands. Kluwer Law Interna tional.

Wall, E. &, Pulitzer, L.(2009). *Stolen innocence: My sto- ry of growing up in a polygamous sect, becoming a teenage bride, and breaking free of Warren Jeffs.* New York N.Y. Harper Collins.

Wampold, B. E. (2001). *The great psychotherapy debate: models, methods, and findings.* Mahwah N.J. Law rence Earlbaum Associates Publishers.

Williams, E. (1944). *Capitalism & Slavery* Chapel Hill, NC: The University of North Carolina

Williams, C. (1987). *The destruction of black civilization, Great issues of a race 4.500 B.C to 2000 A.D.* Chi cago IL: Third World Press.

Woodson, C. (1933). *The miseducation of the Negro.* SanDiego, CA: The Book Tree Publishers

Wundt, W. M. (1904). *Principles of physiological psy chology, Volume 1.* New York. The Macmillan Co.

Zelizer, Viviana. (1985). *Pricing the Priceless Child: The Changing Social Values of Children* Princeton N.J. Princeton University Press. *July.* New York NY: Palgrave Macmillan.

www.ingramcontent.com/pod-product-compliance
Lightning Source LLC
Chambersburg PA
CBHW071954070426
42453CB00008BA/535